ON THE JOB SERIES

REAL PEOPLE WORKING *in*

SERVICE BUSINESSES

Blythe Camenson

Printed on recyclable paper

VGM Career Horizons
a division of *NTC Publishing Group*
Lincolnwood, Illinois USA

Library of Congress Cataloging-in-Publication Data
Camenson, Blythe.
    Real people working in service businesses / Blythe Camenson.
       p.   cm.—(On the job)
    Includes bibliographical references (p.).
    ISBN 0-8442-4732-4.—ISBN 0-8442-4733-2 (pbk.)
    1. Service industries workers—United States.   I. Title.
  II. Series.
  HD8039.S452U62   1997
  331.7'02—dc20

                                                                 96-27790
                                                                  CIP

Published by VGM Career Horizons, a division of NTC Publishing Group
4255 West Touhy Avenue
Lincolnwood (Chicago), Illinois 60646-1975, U.S.A.

6 7 8 9 0 VL 9 8 7 6 5 4 3 2 1

Dedication

To my local police officers and firefighters who protect me; to my
hair stylist who strives to transform me; to all the pilots and crew
who transport me safely; and most of all to my favorite postal
workers who try to bring me good news every day.

Contents

Acknowledgments

The author would like to thank the following professionals for providing information about their careers:

- Gracie Anderson, flight attendant

- Rob Brantley, extrication specialist

- Vivian Portela Buscher, travel agent

- Jim Carr, pilot

- Frank Cassisa, personal trainer

- LeAnne Coury, assistant director of sales

- Laura Craycraft, waitress

- Nick Delia, letter carrier

- Linda Dickinson, chef and menu planner

- Rick Fitzgerald, deputy sheriff

- Samantha Kievman, firefighter

- Robin Landry, esthetician

- Mary Fallon Miller, travel agent

- Jerry O'Brien, engineer

- Elsa Riehl, post office window clerk

- Karen Seals, air traffic controller

- Michael Silvestri, hair stylist

- Missy Soleau, food and beverage manager

About the Author

As a full-time writer of career books, Blythe Camenson's main concern is helping job seekers make educated choices. She firmly believes that with enough information, readers can find long-term, satisfying careers. To that end, she researches traditional as well as unusual occupations, talking to a variety of professionals about what their jobs are really like. In all of her books, she includes first-hand accounts from people who can reveal what to expect in each occupation–the upsides as well as the down.

Camenson's interests range from history and photography to writing novels. She is also director of Fiction Writer's Connection, a membership organization providing support to new and published writers.

Camenson was educated in Boston, earning her B.A. in English and psychology from the University of Massachusetts and her MEd in counseling from Northeastern University.

In addition to *On the Job: Real People Working in Service Businesses,* the other books she has written for VGM Career Horizons are:

Career Portraits: Travel

Career Portraits: Writing

Career Portraits: Nursing

Career Portraits: Firefighting

Careers for History Buffs

Careers for Plant Lovers

Careers for Health Nuts

Careers for Mystery Buffs

Great Jobs for Communications Majors

On the Job: Real People Working in Health Care

Opportunities in Museums

Opportunities in Teaching English to Speakers of Other Languages

How to Use This Book

On the Job: Real People Working in Service Businesses is part of a series designed to serve as companion books to the *Occupational Outlook Handbook (OOH)*. The *OOH* is a useful reference book for librarians, guidance and career counselors, and job seekers. It provides information on hundreds of careers, focusing on the following subjects:

Nature of the work

Working conditions

Employment

Training, other qualifications, and advancement

Job outlook

Earnings

Related occupations

Sources of additional information

What the *OOH* doesn't provide is a first-hand look at what any particular job is really like. That's where the *On the Job* series picks up the slack. In addition to providing an overview of each field and a discussion of the training and education requirements, salary expectations, related fields, and sources to pursue for further information, *On the Job* authors have interviewed dozens of professionals and experts in the various fields.

These first-hand accounts describe what each job truly entails, what the duties are, what the lifestyle is like, and what the upsides and downsides are. The professionals we've spoken with reveal why they were drawn to the field and how they got started in it. And in order to help you make the best career choice for yourself, each professional offers you expert advice based on years of personal experience.

Each chapter also lets you see at a glance, with easy to reference symbols, the level of education and salary range required for the featured occupations.

So, how do you use this book? It's easy. You don't need to run to the library or buy a copy of the *OOH*. All you need to do is glance through our extensive table of contents, find the fields that interest you, and read what the experts have to say.

Introduction to the Field

The service industry leads all other fields as the largest employer in the United States. If you're reading this book, chances are you're already considering a career in one of the many areas of this vast occupational category. Glancing through the Table of Contents will give you an idea of all the choices open to you.

Perhaps you're not sure of the working conditions the different fields offer or which area would best suit your personality, skills, and lifestyle. There are several factors to consider when deciding which sector of the service industry to pursue. Each field carries with it different levels of responsibility and commitment. To identify occupations that will match your expectations, you need to know what each job entails.

Ask yourself the following questions and make note of your answers. Then, as you go through the following chapters, compare your requirements to the information provided by the professionals interviewed in this book. Their comments will help you pinpoint the fields that would interest you, and eliminate those that would clearly be the wrong choice.

- How much of a "people person" are you? Do you prefer to work face to face with clients or customers, or are you more comfortable with telephone contact?

- Do you want a desk job, or would you prefer to be out and about, traveling or covering a police beat or rushing to the scene of a fire? Some occupations offer more challenge–and danger–than others.

- How much time are you willing to commit to training? Some skills can be learned on-the-job or in a year or two of formal training; others can take considerably longer.

- How much money do you expect to earn after you graduate and after you have a few years' experience under your belt?

Salaries and earnings vary greatly in each chosen service profession.

- How much independence do you require? Do you want to be your own boss or will you be content as a salaried employee?

- Will you work normal hours? Or will your day start at 5:30 A.M. and not end until 13 or 14 hours later? Can you handle emergency calls in the middle of the night? Do you want to have your weekends free?

- How much stress can you handle? Would you prefer to avoid work that could be emotional draining?

Knowing what your expectations are, then comparing them to the realities of the work, will help you make informed choices.

If you still have questions after reading this book, there are a number of other avenues to pursue. You can find out more information by contacting the sources listed at the end of each chapter. You can also find professionals on your own to talk to and observe as they go about their work. Any remaining gaps you discover can be filled by referring to the *Occupational Outlook Handbook.*

CHAPTER 1 Firefighting

EDUCATION
H.S. Required
On-the-Job Training Possible
A.A./A.S. Recommended

$$$ SALARY/EARNINGS
$12,000 to $50,000

OVERVIEW

Today's firefighters are brave and dedicated men and women who love the challenge and satisfaction of helping people in trouble. They risk their lives every day to save victims trapped in burning buildings, pull children out of wrecked cars, battle forest fires, or contain dangerous chemicals that have spilled and are threatening lives or the environment.

Firefighters are a special breed. They are go-getters, team players, and strong-minded individuals who know how to get a job done and done well.

Because most fire departments combine firefighting with rescue services, calls come in that can involve anything from car wrecks and heart attacks to kitchen fires and full warehouse blazes.

Firefighters need to be prepared to handle any type of call. They work odd hours, usually a 24-hour shift, with 48 or 72 hours off between. During that 24-hour period they are on call and can never really relax. The tones can start sounding at any time–in the middle of a meal, during a training session, or late at night when they're fast asleep in the dorm.

Because of the emergencies and traumas these people share, firefighters feel very close to their co-workers. Most firefighters will tell you that being on the job is like being with a close-knit family, with brothers and sisters all working together.

Although shift work can be grueling, there is a lot of time off between shifts. Firefighters put this time to good use, furthering their education or working at second jobs. You'll find firefighters who are also lawyers, teachers, private investigators, funeral directors, swimming pool remodelers, and everything else in between.

Teamwork is the most important aspect of being a firefighter. This is not a job for loners. Their lives and the lives of others depend on cooperation and trust. On a team, the nozzle man can't put water on the fire unless the engineer makes it happen, and that doesn't happen unless the mechanic has done his job, and so on. Every person has a role to play.

TRAINING FOR FIREFIGHTERS

Gone are the days when a kid fresh out of high school can walk in the door and say "Here I am, how 'bout a job?" In the past fire departments would take you on and train you. The pay was low and it was dangerous work; not that many people wanted to become firefighters.

These days there is much more competition and most fire departments expect you to have undergone training before you even apply for a job.

If you're serious about working as a firefighter, the best way is to get some training first. You can take a 12-week firefighter training program (usually offered at community colleges) or study in a two-year program for an associate's degree in fire science.

Once hired, firefighters continue their training, either on their own or through in-house classes. They need to keep their skills current, and there are many specialties to learn as well.

It is also important to have good verbal and written skills. Firefighters are often called on to speak in front of groups, and they must be adept at writing reports. Math and chemistry are important too, and those who want to climb the administrative ladder should take business and management courses.

Academics are only one part of it, however. Firefighting requires physical and emotional strength. Firefighters wear heavy gear and carry weighty equipment–and regularly run across upsetting situations. Being able to cope is a necessity.

To further enhance your chances of being employed, it's a good idea to try to get some related experience first. Volunteer fire departments still make up a large percentage of our country's firefighting force. They usually will accept trainees who are still in school. The Boy Scouts of America also has a program to train future firefighters.

RANKS AND DIVISIONS

The firefighting service is run in quasi-military fashion. There are rules and regulations to follow, uniforms, roll call, assigned duties, and a ranking system.

Here is a list of the different divisions you will find in a fire department.

Operations

Fire and Safety Inspection/Public Education

Fire Investigation

Emergency Medical Services

Training

Administration

No matter in which division you work you will have a rank. The titles and, sometimes, the specific duties vary from department to department but the general responsibilities are the same.

Combat Firefighter

This is the rank that everyone starts out with. Many people are content to stay at that rank, while others work toward promotion and continue to move up the ladder. Firefighters do just as their title implies–they fight fires. They might also learn specialties and deal with hazardous materials or medical emergencies.

Driver/Engineer

This person is responsible for getting the crew and equipment to the scene. The driver/engineer dispenses tools and makes sure there is enough of a water supply.

Lieutenant

This is a first-level supervisory position. The lieutenant is responsible for the station during his or her shift, making sure that it's run properly, to assign duties, and to ensure the welfare and safety of his crew.

Battalion Chief/Captain/Division Chief/Commander

Division chiefs command the following different departments:

TRAINING.   The chief is responsible for maintaining continuing education units for both firefighters and EMS personnel.

RESOURCE MANAGEMENT DIVISION/SUPPORT SERVICES/PURCHASING.   The chief is responsible for every item purchased, all the equipment and day-to-day supplies, he or she is also responsible for the maintenance of fire/rescue vehicles.

FIRE PREVENTION/PUBLIC EDUCATION.   The chief oversees fire inspectors and all programs dealing with the public. This division is also responsible for generating revenue through inspection fees the city charges.

EMERGENCY MEDICAL SERVICE (EMS).   This division is responsible for all the emergency medical care given on the different shifts. The head of EMS monitors personnel, vacations and days off, and scheduling, and must see to it that all the vehicles have the right amount of crew and paramedics.

OPERATIONS.   Operations is responsible for all the firefighting shifts. The duties are similar see to those of the EMS division head.

   In smaller departments with smaller budgets the divisions are sometimes combined and a division head will be responsible for more than one area of operation.

Supervisors

Many departments also have supervisors who report directly to division heads. They might supervise the hour-by-hour activities of a shift; often they follow the trucks out on calls, driving in their own specially marked cars.

Deputy Chief/Assistant Chief

Some cities or municipalities have only one deputy chief, who is responsible for all the different divisions within the organization. Other cities could have several assistants or deputies, each responsible for a different division.

In the absence of the fire chief, the ultimate responsibility rests on the deputy chief. He or she will take over the day-to-day command, or will represent the department, attending meetings in the chief's place.

Fire Chief

The fire chief is in charge of the entire firefighting organization. That organization could encompass an entire county or city, with several fire stations located throughout the zone.

In a nutshell, the fire chief is ultimately responsible for everything. He or she works with whatever government body is responsible for fire and rescue functions, planning services and seeing that the plans are put into action. For example, a fire system might aim for a three-minute response time on paramedic calls and five minutes on fire calls. It's the fire chief's job to make sure that plan works. Essentially, the chief must manage the organization and its resources, personnel and equipment to meet the goals established by the city.

The chief is also expected to be the ultimate professional expert in the field. The fire chief can be appointed by a government official but, as is more and more common, he or she will have been a career firefighter who has gone through the ranks.

CAREER PATHS

Once on the force, you have a number of options open to you, and you don't have to be promoted to driver/engineer or lieutenant to take advantage of them. To get on a specialist team you first have to exhibit a desire to do the work. Then there has to be an opening on a particular team. Even more important, the team has to feel you would make a good addition to its ranks. Members would have to trust you and have confidence in your ability to learn.

In addition, each team would require certain training or skills. Here is a list of the different specialty teams you could train for:

Extrication Specialist

These specialists know how to operate the Jaws of Life, a valuable tool for cutting victims trapped in car wrecks.

Training is acquired in a number of ways. Those interested can take courses and seminars offered by rescue equipment manufacturers, learn on the job, or practice on junk cars on their own time. They have to be familiar with levers and hydraulics and understand automobile construction, knowing where both the weak and strong points are.

High-Angle Rescue

These rescuers know how to use ropes and ladders and work at heights above two stories. They may have to rappel off tall buildings where ladders won't reach, or climb up on water tanks or down dangerous cliffsides.

The specialized skills used in high-angle rescues are learned through local fire academies or community colleges and through on-the-job training. Obviously, potential high-angle team members cannot be afraid of heights. They must have steady nerves and, as all firefighters must, they should be in good physical condition.

Hazardous Materials Technician

This specialty is commonly known as "Haz-Mat." Haz-Mat technicians are familiar with all sorts of chemicals and their containers. They also learn about valves and plumbing and patching. Whenever there's an accident or a spill and these materials pose a public risk, Haz-Mat firefighters step in.

Haz-Mat trainees study chemicals and how they behave when spilled or involved in a fire. They learn how to use heat detectors and monitors, as well as how to use computers to help in researching and identifying different chemicals. Programs are offered through fire academies, community colleges, and through continuing education courses given at individual fire departments. Because new chemicals are constantly turning up on the market, study is an ongoing process.

Technical Rescue

Technical rescue includes underground rescue in confined spaces. Urban search and rescue specialists are experts in finding people in the aftermath of hurricanes or earthquakes, when buildings have collapsed, trapping them under piles of rubble. Technical rescuers also know how to pull out a dog or other animal trapped in a well or drain pipe.

Techniques for technical rescues are taught in fire academies, community college fire science programs, and during in-house continuing education training.

Underwater Rescue

Underwater rescue teams are trained to dive in the ocean, in lakes, and into dark canals. They know how to operate with zero visibility, feeling their way along the bottom with their hands, searching for a submerged car or body.

These experts are all trained as certified divers. They have to be expert swimmers first, with strength and endurance. In addition to the skills every scuba diver learns, underwater rescue divers must know how to work in pitch black conditions, in freezing water, or in dangerous rapids or heavy surf conditions. They must also be familiar with various equipment, such as grappling hooks or inflatable boats.

Emergency Medical Services

Emergency medical technicians and paramedics are versed in all sorts of medical emergencies. Their role and the training they receive is covered in depth in *On the Job: Real People Working in Health and Medicine*.

ADVANCEMENT

It is important for future administrators to develop good writing, speaking, and reading skills. In today's fire service, candidates for promotion take a civil service exam that tests written skills, reading comprehension, and technical knowledge.

Your verbal skills will also be tested in an oral interview format, and specific administrative skills will be assessed in role-playing activities. You will be judged on how you make tactical decisions in firefighting situations; how you perform with "in-basket/out-basket" exercises and handle administrative situations; and how you deal with personnel problems.

Ongoing employee evaluations and recommendations from your supervisors will also play a part in whether or not you are promoted.

Many of the specific skills you will need to move up the ladder can be developed on the job. Assist your supervisors with their duties and take business and management courses when they are offered.

JOB OUTLOOK

In most areas of the country, the number of qualified applicants generally exceeds the number of job openings, even though the written examination and physical requirements eliminate many applicants. This situation is expected to persist through the year 2005.

Employment of firefighters is expected to increase about as fast as the average for all occupations through the year 2005, as a result of the increase in the nation's population and fire protection needs.

In addition, the number of paid firefighter positions is expected to increase as a percentage of all firefighter jobs. Much of the expected increase will occur in smaller communities with expanding populations that augment volunteers with career firefighters to better meet, increasingly complex fireprotection needs. However, little growth is expected in large urban fire departments. A small number of local governments are expected to contract for firefighting services with private companies.

Turnover of firefighter jobs is unusually low, particularly for an occupation that requires a relatively limited investment in formal education. Nevertheless, most job openings are expected to result from the need to replace those who retire or transfer to other occupations.

Layoffs of firefighters are not common. Fire protection is an essential service, and citizens are likely to exert considerable pressure on city officials to expand or at least preserve the level of fire-protection coverage. Even when there are budget cuts, local fire departments usually cut expenses by postponing equipment purchases or not hiring new firefighters rather than by laying off staff.

SALARIES

As with any profession, salaries vary depending upon the region of the country and the size of the department's budget. Generally speaking, firefighters can start anywhere from the high teens to $40,000 a year or more. The salaries are very attractive at the highest levels. Fire chiefs can earn between $85,000 and $100,000 a year, and sometimes even more. There are regular raises, and salaries increase with the special skills you learn.

Some departments are able to reward firefighters with bonuses for years of service or give merit increases when they earn an outstanding evaluation. The more degrees and certifications you have, the more money you will make.

RELATED FIELDS

One occupation related to firefighting is the fire-protection engineer, who identifies fire hazards in homes and workplaces, and designs prevention programs and automatic fire detection and extinguishing systems. Other occupations in which workers respond to emergencies include police officers (see Chapter 3) and paramedics and emergency medical technicians. (See information earlier in this chapter and *On the Job: Real People Working in Health and Medicine*.)

INTERVIEW

Samantha Kievman
Firefighter

Samantha Kievman is a firefighter, an Emergency Medical Technician

(EMT) and a paramedic. She has been with her fire department since 1993.

What the Job's Really Like

"In the fire service you see it all and you do it all. You get to meet so many people and you're always surrounded by people. When you pull up on scene they're so happy to see you. It's great.

"We go on so many calls. All sorts of fires–cars, houses, kitchens. There are also medical calls–slip and falls or chest pains or car accidents. Anything you can imagine.

"The work is challenging and different. You never know what to expect. When you come into work you have to be on the alert for 24 hours. No matter what you're doing, you have to stop to go on a call–and you'll never know what it will be. The call could be for a simple slip and fall, but when you get there the guy is having chest pains. We might have a quiet day, or a day where we're running 24 hours straight without stopping.

"When we're not out on a call, we have station duties. One day a week we take everything out of the kitchen, mop the floors, wipe down the walls, clean out the refrigerators, clean the stove–it's a lot more than I do at my own house. Another day we clean out the dorm, put up all the beds, wipe them down, vacuum. On Saturday it's lawn day and we do all our own lawn maintenance. And if something goes wrong at the station, we fix it. Every day there's something to do.

"We also have training sessions. We watch training videos or take classes–Haz-Mat technician training, EMT refresher courses, and paramedic meetings once a month.

"It's a great job, but there are some downsides. There's a lot of pressure when you pull up on a car accident and you've got four victims and they're all hurt badly. You're running around and there are 20 people on scene and everyone's doing something.

"And if someone dies, it's terrible. Although we'd like to, we can't save everybody. You kind of have to make yourself cold to it. If you let it bother you, you can't do your job. You have to have compassion, but you also have to put up a little wall so you can handle the job and go back for your next 24-hour shift."

How Samantha Kievman Got Started

"Before I even applied for a job, I went to a community college to become an EMT first. That took one semester. When I finished that, I attended a local fire training academy for another 12 weeks. When I started working as a firefighter, I also attended paramedic school.

"Training starts first thing in the morning and finishes up at six or so at night, five days a week for twelve weeks. Every morning you run a mile and a half, do sit ups and pull ups–all sorts of different work outs.

"Then you get cleaned up and go into the classroom and work with textbooks. We review something in class and then we go outside and actually do it. If it was a hose lay, we'd get bunkered out (put our gear on) and do a hose lay. If it was something to do with ladders, we'd go outside and get the ladders out.

"In a training facility they would sometimes smoke up a room and we'd put our air bottles on. There'd be flares set up to indicate where the fire was. We'd have to ladder the building and climb up to the second floor, bring up the hose line, open it up, and flow water. Everything is as realistic as possible.

"Not everyone makes it through the training program. Either they can't keep up physically or academically. I came home and studied every night. It's exhausting. You're climbing and lugging heavy dummies and equipment. It's physically and mentally demanding.

"When I took my state tests–the written and the practical–I felt really confident. I had studied and put a lot of time into it."

Expert Advice

"Go for it! Go to EMT school, go to paramedic school, go through fire school, get as much schooling as you possibly can. Some fire departments won't even accept your application unless you're EMT and firefighting certified.

"The fire service wants someone who's going to put in 100 percent. We're dealing with people's lives. You don't want second best. You want top notch people."

INTERVIEW
Jerry O'Brien
Driver/Engineer

Jerry O'Brien is a driver/engineer as well as a Haz-Mat technician. He has been a firefighter since 1982 and has worked for two different fire departments on opposite ends of the country. He has taken the test for lieutenant and is number one on the list. He expects to get promoted this year.

What the Job's Really Like

"You have to maintain the apparatus and equipment. You do a daily bumper to bumper inspection of every piece of equipment that's on board to make sure it's all in working order. All the medical gear has to be inspected, all the tools have to be in a state of readiness, there has to be oil, gas, and water in the truck, and you have to make sure the hose lines are correct.

"The next thing you are responsible for is transporting the firefighters and the crew to whatever assignment you've received. It could be a medical call or a fire or going to a train wreck. You could be driving in a lot of traffic.

"At a fire you are responsible for supplying water for the fire suppression–establishing enough water coming into the engine from the hydrant and pumping it out to the structure.

"Once the water is flowing, the engineer has to make sure it doesn't fall off. If it did fall off, the firefighters' lives would be in extreme danger. You're also responsible for dispensing all of the tools on the apparatus, the axes, pry bars, whatever is needed. Or you might start up a generator and bring lights into the scene. The engineer is the one in the crew who's making all of the parts come together at the fire scene.

"The fun thing about being an engineer is getting to drive a big truck. I've driven fire engines in the mountains, on ice, and on all kinds of terrain. And you're handling a million things at once. It's a challenge. But once you get to the fire you get a good feeling from everything running smoothly.

"The tough part is that you don't get to go into the fire. It's hard to sit there and watch your buddies put on their air packs and go in to attack a fire. I was a firefighter before, and this job is a promotion, but it takes you out of the heat for a while. Literally. And you don't get back into that position until you get promoted again to lieutenant.

"A lot of us are in this because it's fun to put out a fire. It's like going into combat or playing football."

How Jerry O'Brien Got Started

"I didn't anticipate getting into the fire service; I stumbled upon it by accident. I was managing a retail store, working 70 or 80 hours a week, killing myself. I saw an ad in the paper for the fire department. I went through the physical and written testing and then I got hired after about a year and a half on the waiting list. Once I got into the fire service I found out that firefighters study a lot–they actually go to college, and learn fire behavior, rescue techniques, high-angle rescue. I found it fascinating.

"To become an engineer in most fire departments you must have at least three years as a firefighter. During that time you study books and manuals on water flow, the apparatus itself, and driving in hazardous conditions. You really need to know your equipment.

"There's a written test and a practical test. You hook up to a hydrant and are given a couple of problems. For example, you're told to stretch a one and three quarters-inch hose and a two and half-inch hose and flow them at the correct water pressures. You have to be able to go to the pump panel and make split-second calculations, and then operate the apparatus in such a way that doesn't over pressure a line. People will be on the end of that line.

"The practical portion of the exam is a real challenge. You need a knowledge of basic math and algebra and how to use hydraulic formulas. You have to know how to plug the numbers in. Some of the newer trucks actually will do a lot of the calculating for you and will have flow meters on the truck for you. Technology has simplified the job.

Expert Advice

"Education is crucial these days. You should think about earning a college degree–in EMS and fire science–because that knowledge is becoming more and more important. There aren't many bachelor degree programs now; it's mainly at the associate's level, but in coming years there will be more and more four-year programs.

"And when opportunities present themselves to learn new skills, through your organization or on your own, take advantage of it. You need to grow and to learn more than your job."

INTERVIEW

Rob Brantley
Extrication Specialist

Rob Brantley has been a firefighter since 1975. In addition to being an extrication specialist, he is also an EMT and is part of several other specialty teams.

What the Job's Really Like

"I go out on fires–houses or cars or boats. You can't imagine the different things that can catch on fire. Warehouses are the most dangerous because you don't know what's inside. There could be gunpowder or chemicals.

"I also go out on any kind of auto accident. We'll get a Signal Four, which is an accident, usually with injuries. We go there to stabilize the situation, remove any danger to life or property. For example, if the car crashes into a house and the car is burning, we try to get the car out of the way so the house doesn't catch too.

"I've seen some dreadful accidents. It bothers you, especially if you can't get someone out in time or it was too bad of a wreck and there was nothing you could do. And it can particularly bother you if it's a bad wreck with kids in it. It stays with me for a long time.

"We also do all kinds of medical and other kinds of rescues. But we don't often rescue cats from trees. If you think about it, you don't often see cat skeletons in trees–they always manage to get themselves down.

"We've rescued quite a few pelicans out of trees, though. They get caught in fishing lines, then fly up into the trees and the line gets caught.

"We've also rescued dogs out of sewer pipes and have gone out in the ocean for boat rescues. If a boat capsizes, we might get called before the Coast Guard and that's when our dive team can go to work. We have a Zodiac, an inflatable boat, and a surf boat we can use to paddle out to the people.

"Working the Jaws of Life is my favorite thing to do. If someone is in trouble at a wreck, I like to feel I can get them out faster than anyone. I've spent a lot of time practicing taking cars apart."

How Rob Brantley Got Started

"I always wanted to be a firefighter; in fact, no other job possibility had ever crossed my mind. In addition to my formal firefighting training, I went to some seminars, but most of my specialty training is from general knowledge. I worked with hydraulics before I got on the fire department. It's kind of a 'give me a lever, I can move the world' feeling. It seems to come naturally to me. It has to be in you–it's hard to force that stuff. If you want to get trained, most departments will train you.

"Everyone is exposed to all the different specialties, and if you want, you can go out of your way to practice. You can tell your supervisor you'd like to go over to the junkyard and practice taking cars apart.

"After the probation period, you can start investigating the teams in your department. But the crew has to have confidence in you. The person in charge of the team will take a poll–'Do you know such and such? What do you think? Could he or she do the job? Should we give them a try?'

"The teams are dangerous so you don't want someone next to you who's going to panic. Then you'll just have one more person to rescue.

Expert Advice

"To be an extrication specialist, you need common sense and you have to know about leverage and about how different parts of the cars will react to pressure. What will bend, what won't bend.

"There are parts of a car that are structurally less strong than others. You've got to know where and how to cut. You have to know how to take windshields out without getting glass all over everybody. Safety is the key. You don't want to hurt the person in the car anymore than he's already been hurt; you don't want to hurt anybody that's standing around you.

"Also, there's a time factor. They call it the 'Golden Hour.' Basically, you have an hour to get someone out of a wreck and to a trauma center to increase their chances of survival. You have to know how to act fast. You could make it worse if you pushed on the wrong part of the car; you could crush the person inside."

● ● ●

FOR MORE INFORMATION

The Boy Scouts of America has a great program for both boys and girls to learn about careers in firefighting. Through the Exploring Program, local fire departments will work with teens, provide them with uniforms, and teach them the basics of firefighting.

Once a week they meet as a group with professional firefighters who are coordinating the program. They get general training in first-aid, the fire trucks, and equipment. After they put in a certain number of hours and are tested, they are allowed to ride on the trucks. They are issued fire gear and can go to fires and other emergencies.

Although cadets are not allowed to go into burning buildings, the program is an excellent way to find out what it's really like being a firefighter.

Cadets can start the program at age 14 and stay in until they are 20 years old. Cadets often get hired as full-time firefighters right out of the program.

Boy Scouts of America
Exploring Program
P.O. Box 152079
Irving, TX 75015

International Association of Fire Fighters
1750 New York Avenue, NW
Washington, DC 20006

For additional information on salaries and hours of work for firefighters in various cities, see the *Municipal Yearbook*, published by the International City Management Association. The *Yearbook* is available in most public libraries.

To get an idea about what firefighting exams are like, and even start practicing to get a head start, you can take a look at *Arco Firefighter*, by Robert Andriuolo, Deputy Chief, New York City Fire Department, (Prentice Hall).

This book, which is available in many public libraries, will help prepare you for the different firefighter exams. It reviews all the subject matter you'll need to know, provides sample written and physical fitness tests, and gives tips and strategies for earning high test scores.

For information about professional qualifications and a list of two- and four-year degree programs in fire science or fire prevention contact:

National Fire Protection Association
Batterymarch Park
Quincy, MA 02269

For information about careers as a firefighter trainer write to:

The National Fire Academy
16825 South Seton Avenue
Emmitsburg, MD 21727

For information about administrative careers in firefighting write to:

International Association of Fire Chiefs
4025 Fair Ridge Drive
Fairfax, VA 22033-286

CHAPTER 2 Police Work

EDUCATION
H.S. Required
A.A./A.S. Recommended
B.A./B.S Recommended

$$$ SALARY/EARNINGS
$30,000 to $50,000

OVERVIEW

The safety of our nation's cities, towns, and highways greatly depends on the work of police officers, deputy sheriffs, detectives, and special agents, whose responsibilities range from controlling traffic to preventing and investigating crimes. In most jurisdictions, these officers are expected to exercise their authority whenever necessary, whether they are on or off duty.

As civilian police department employees and private security personnel increasingly assume routine police duties, police and detectives are able to spend more time fighting serious crime. Police and detectives are also becoming more involved in community relations, increasing public confidence in the police and mobilizing the public to help the police fight crime.

Police officers and detectives who work in small communities and rural areas have many duties. In the course of a single day's work, they may direct traffic at the scene of a fire, investigate a burglary, or give first aid to an accident victim. In a large police department, by contrast, officers usually are assigned to a specific type of duty. Most officers are detailed either to patrol or to traffic duty; a smaller number is assigned to special work such as accident prevention. Others are experts in chemical and microscopic analysis, firearms identification, and handwriting and fingerprint identification. In very large cities, a few officers may work with special units, such as mounted and motorcycle police, harbor patrols, helicopter patrols, canine corps, mobile rescue teams, and youth aid services.

Sheriffs and deputy sheriffs generally enforce the law in rural areas or those places where there is no local police department. Bailiffs are responsible for keeping order in the courtroom. U.S. marshals serve civil writs and criminal warrants issued by federal judges and are responsible for the safety and transportation of jurors and prisoners.

Detectives and special agents are plainclothes investigators who gather facts and collect evidence for criminal cases. They conduct interviews, examine records, observe the activities of suspects, and participate in raids or arrests.

Special agents for the Federal Bureau of Investigation (FBI) investigate violations of federal laws in connection with bank robberies, theft of government property, organized crime, espionage, sabotage, kidnapping, and terrorism. Agents with specialized training usually work on cases related to their background. For example, agents with an accounting background may investigate white-collar crimes, such as bank embezzlements or fraudulent bankruptcies and land deals. Frequently, agents must testify in court about cases that they investigate.

Special agents employed by the U.S. Department of Treasury work for the U.S. Customs Service; the Bureau of Alcohol, Tobacco, and Firearms; the U.S. Secret Service; and the Internal Revenue Service. Customs agents enforce laws to prevent smuggling of goods across U.S. borders. Alcohol, Tobacco, and Firearms agents might investigate suspected illegal sales of guns or the underpayment of taxes by a liquor or cigarette manufacturer. U.S. Secret Service agents protect the president, vice president, and their immediate families, presidential candidates, ex-presidents, and foreign dignitaries visiting the United States. Secret Service agents also investigate counterfeiting, the forgery of government checks or bonds, and the fraudulent use of credit cards. Internal Revenue Service special agents collect evidence against individuals and companies that are evading the payment of federal taxes.

Federal drug enforcement agents conduct criminal investigations of illicit drug activity. They compile evidence and arrest individuals who violate federal drug laws. They may prepare reports that are used in criminal proceedings, give testimony in court, and develop evidence that justifies the seizure of financial assets gained from illegal activity.

State police officers (sometimes called state troopers or highway patrol officers) patrol highways and enforce the laws and regulations that govern their use. They issue traffic citations to motorists who violate the law. They direct traffic at the scene of an accident, give first aid, and call for emergency equipment, including ambulances. They also write reports that may be used to determine the cause of the accident. In addition, state police officers provide services to highway motorists. For example, the officers may radio for road service for drivers with mechanical trouble, direct tourists to their destination, or give information about lodging, restaurants, and tourist attractions.

State police officers also provide traffic assistance and control during road repairs, fires, and other emergencies, as well as during special occurrences such as parades and sports events. They sometimes check the weight of commercial vehicles, conduct driver examinations, and give information on highway safety to the public.

In addition to highway responsibilities, state police in the majority of states also enforce criminal laws. In communities and counties that do not have a local police force or a large sheriff's department, the state police are the primary law enforcement agency, investigating crimes such as burglary or assault. They also may help city or county police catch lawbreakers and control civil disturbances.

Most new police recruits begin on patrol duty, riding in a police vehicle or walking on foot patrol. They work alone or with experienced officers in such varied areas as congested business districts or outlying residential neighborhoods. Officers attempt to become thoroughly familiar with conditions throughout their area and, while on patrol, remain alert for anything unusual. They note suspicious circumstances, such as open windows or lights in vacant buildings, as well as hazards to public safety such as burned-out street lights or fallen trees. Officers enforce traffic regulations and also watch for stolen vehicles. At regular intervals, officers report to police headquarters from call boxes, radios, or telephones.

Regardless of where they work, police, detectives, and special agents must write reports and maintain police records. They may be called to testify in court when their arrests result in legal action. Some officers, such as division or bureau chiefs, are responsible for training or certain kinds of criminal investigations; those who command police operations in an assigned area have administrative and supervisory duties.

TRAINING

Civil service regulations govern the appointment of police and detectives in practically all states, as well as in large cities and in many small ones. Candidates must be U.S. citizens, usually at least 20 years of age, and must meet rigorous physical and personal qualifications. Eligibility for appointment depends on performance in competitive written examinations, as well as on education and experience. Physical examinations often include tests of vision, strength, and agility.

Because personal characteristics such as honesty, good judgment, and a sense of responsibility are especially important in police and detective work, candidates are interviewed by a senior officer at police headquarters, and their character traits and background are investigated. In some police departments, candidates also may be interviewed by a psychiatrist or a psychologist, or be given a personality test. Most applicants are subjected to lie detector examinations and drug testing. Some police departments subject police officers in sensitive positions to drug testing as a condition of continuing employment.

In large police departments, where most jobs are found, applicants usually must have a high-school education. An increasing number of cities and states require some college training, and some hire law enforcement students as police interns; some departments require a college degree. A few police departments accept applicants as recruits who have less than a high-school education, particularly if they have worked in a field related to law enforcement.

To be considered for appointment as an FBI special agent, an applicant either must be a graduate of an accredited law school; be a college graduate with a major in either accounting, engineering, or computer science; or be a college graduate with either fluency in a foreign language or 3 years of full-time work experience. Applicants must be U.S. citizens, between 23 and 35 years of age at the time of appointment, and willing to accept an assignment anywhere in the United States. They also must be in excellent physical condition with at least 20/200 vision corrected to 20/40 in one eye and 20/20 in the other eye. All new agents undergo 15 weeks of training at the FBI academy at the U.S. Marine Corps base in Quantico, Virginia.

Applicants for special agent jobs with the U.S. Department of Treasury must have a bachelor's degree, or a minimum of three years' work experience–with at least two years in criminal investigation. Candidates must be in excellent physical condition and be less than 35 years of age at the time they enter duty. Treasury agents undergo eight weeks of training at the Federal Law Enforcement Training Center in Glynco, Georgia, and another eight weeks of specialized training with their particular bureau.

Applicants for special agent jobs with the U.S. Drug Enforcement Administration must have a college degree in any field and either one year of experience conducting criminal investigations or have achieved a record of scholastic excellence while in college. The minimum age for entry is 21 and the maximum age is 36. Drug enforcement agents undergo 14 weeks of specialized training at the FBI Academy in Quantico, Virginia.

More and more, police departments are encouraging applicants to take post-high school training in law enforcement. Many entrants to police and detective jobs have completed some formal postsecondary education; a significant number are college graduates. Many junior colleges, colleges, and universities offer programs in law enforcement or administration of justice. Other courses helpful in preparing for a police career include psychology, counseling, English, American history, public administration, public relations, sociology, business law, chemistry, and physics. Participation in physical education and sports is especially helpful in developing the stamina and agility needed for police work. Knowledge of a foreign language is an asset in areas that have concentrations of ethnic populations.

Some large cities hire high-school graduates who are still in their teens as civilian police cadets or trainees. They do clerical work and attend classes, and are appointed to the regular force at age 21 if they qualify.

Before their first assignments, officers usually go through a period of training. In small communities, recruits work for a short time with experienced officers. In state and large city police departments, they get more formal training that may last a number of weeks or months. This training includes classroom instruction in constitutional law and civil rights, state laws and local ordinances, and accident investigation. Recruits also receive training and supervised experience in patrol, traffic control, use of firearms, self-defense, first aid, and handling emergencies.

Police officers usually become eligible for promotion after a probationary period ranging from six months to three years. In a large department, promotion may enable an officer to become a detective or specialize in one type of police work, such as laboratory analysis of evidence, traffic control, communications, or working with juveniles. Promotions to sergeant, lieutenant, and captain usually are made according to a candidate's position on a promotion list, as determined by scores on a written examination and on-the-job performance.

Many types of training help police officers and detectives improve their job performance. Through annual required training given at police department academies in many states and colleges, officers keep abreast of crowd-control techniques, civil defense, legal developments that affect their work, and advances in law enforcement equipment. Many police departments pay all or part of the tuition for officers to work toward associate and bachelor's degrees in law enforcement, police science, administration of justice, or public administration. Those who earn a degree are usually paid a higher salary.

JOB OUTLOOK

Employment of police officers, detectives, and special agents is expected to increase more slowly than the average for all occupations through the year 2005. A more security-conscious society, and growing concern about drug-related crimes, should contribute to the increasing demand for police services. However, employment growth will be tempered somewhat by the continuing budgetary constraints faced by law enforcement agencies. In addition, private security firms may increasingly assume some routine police duties, such as crowd surveillance at airports and other public places. Although turnover in police, detective, and special agent jobs is among the lowest of all occupations, the need to replace workers who retire, transfer to other occupations, or stop working for other reasons will be the source of most job openings.

The opportunity for public service through police work is attractive to many. The job frequently is challenging and involves much responsibility. Furthermore, in many communities, police officers may retire with a pension to pursue a second career while still in their 40s. Because police officers receive attractive salaries and benefits, the number of qualified candidates generally exceeds the number of job openings in many federal agencies and some state and local police departments, resulting in increased hiring standards and selectivity by employers. Competition is expected to remain keen for higher-paying jobs in larger police departments. Those with college training in law enforcement should have the best opportunities, and job potential will be best in those communities whose departments are expanding and are having difficulty attracting an adequate supply of police officers.

Competition is expected to be extremely keen for special agent positions with the FBI, Treasury Department, and Drug Enforcement Administration, as these prestigious jobs tend to attract a far greater number of applicants than the number of job openings. Consequently, only the most highly qualified candidates will obtain jobs.

The level of government spending influences the employment of police officers, detectives, and special agents. The number of job opportunities, therefore, can vary from year to year and from place to place. Layoffs, on the other hand, are rare; early retirements enable most staffing cuts to be handled through attrition. Police officers who lose their jobs from budget cuts usually have little difficulty finding jobs with other police departments.

SALARIES

In 1992 the median salary of nonsupervisory police officers and detectives was about $32,000 a year. The middle 50 percent earned between about $24,500 and $41,200; the lowest paid 10 percent were paid less than $18,400, while the highest paid 10 percent earned over $51,200 a year. Generally, salaries tend to be higher in larger, more urban jurisdictions, which usually have bigger police departments.

Police officers and detectives in supervisory positions had a median salary of about $38,100 a year, also in 1992. The middle 50 percent earned between about $28,300 and $49,800; the lowest paid 10 percent were paid less than $23,200, while the highest paid 10 percent earned over $58,400 annually.

Sheriffs, bailiffs, and other law enforcement officers had a median annual salary of about $25,800 in 1992. The middle 50 percent earned between about $20,500 and $30,900; the lowest paid 10 percent were paid less than $15,600, while the highest paid 10 percent earned over $38,800.

In 1993 FBI agents started at about $30,600 a year, while Treasury Department agents started at about $18,300 or $22,700 a year, and DEA agents at either $22,700 or $27,800 a year, depending on their qualifications. Salaries of experienced FBI agents in the FBI started at around $47,900, while supervisory agents in the FBI started at around $56,600 a year. Salaries of experienced Treasury Department and DEA agents started at $40,200, while supervisory agents in this department started at $47,900. Federal agents may, however, be eligible for a special law enforcement compensation and retirement plan; applicants should ask their recruiter for more information.

Total earnings frequently exceed the stated salary due to payments for overtime, which can be significant, especially during criminal investigations or when police are needed for crowd control during sporting events or political rallies. In addition to the common fringe benefits–paid vacation, sick leave, and medical and life insurance–most police departments and federal agencies provide officers with special allowances for uniforms, and furnish revolvers, nightsticks, handcuffs, and other required equipment. In addition, because police officers generally are covered by liberal pension plans, many retire at half-pay after 20 or 25 years of service.

RELATED FIELDS

Police officers are called upon to maintain law and order in the nation's cities, towns, and rural areas. Workers in related law enforcement occupations include guards, bailiffs, correction officers, fire marshals, and fish and game wardens.

INTERVIEW

Rick Fitzgerald
Deputy Sheriff

Rick Fitzgerald is a deputy sheriff with the Broward County Sheriff's Office in South Florida. He has been doing police work since 1986.

What the Job's Really Like

"Although the duties of the Sheriff's Office might differ from state to state, in Broward County we handle the jails, we handle all civil injunctions–evictions, serving restraining orders–we handle the unincorporated areas, and we also handle what we call 'contract cities.' Some cities in the county, rather than hiring their own police department, discover they can save money by contracting with the sheriff directly. That happened to me. I worked for the City of Tamarac Police Department, then one day I came in and found that the city had contracted with the Sheriff's Office to take over the police work. My job stayed the same, I just had to wear a different uniform.

"I work in road patrol, which is basically what your normal street policeman does. It involves answering calls, working traffic accidents, traffic enforcement, writing tickets, and stuff like that. Fortunately for me, I work in a quiet city.

"Probably one thing a lot of people fail to see–or they don't know until they get into this line of work–is the amount of paperwork a police officer does. A lot of paperwork is generated for all the different types of calls, and sometimes you find yourself writing up meaningless reports. People need reports to go to court or for an insurance claim, but these reports are often for things that really aren't police matters. But we have to get involved because other concerns require these reports.

"I've handled just about anything you can imagine. I've taken all kinds of strange reports, all the way from something meaningless to a very serious call. Here's an example of what I mean by a meaningless call: A few months ago a lady came in to tell me she lost her hearing aid. I told her that there were no serial numbers on hearing aids, that there was nothing we could trace or track to her. A police report is not warranted here, you don't need a police report. She didn't know that at the time and she said okay and left. But lo and behold, she came back to me three weeks later and said, 'Look, I *do* need you to make a report. I realize it's ridiculous, but my insurance company won't pay me the $400 for the hearing aid unless I give them a police report.' Sometimes we end up feeling like glorified secretaries.

"Traffic accidents are another example. Minor traffic accidents where there are no criminal offenses shouldn't be a police matter. It's a civil matter to begin with and unless there's a crime involved–the driver's license had been suspended, or it's a Driving Under the Influence case or there are any injuries–we shouldn't have to be involved. But the report we end up having to write is just for the insurance company. It can take up an hour of our time.

"I work eight-hour days, five on, two off. I spend all eight hours on the road, and so I have to do all the paperwork in my car on a clipboard. And you hope that you have time between your calls to get all the paperwork done. Today, for example, I was extremely busy and I just went from one call to another.

"During the course of the day I went to a bank for two different forgeries–someone had stolen some checks and forged signatures. I also had a call for a runaway juvenile, so that right there are three reports that I have to sit and try to write in between my other duties.

"In road patrol your job entails everything. They expect you to handle your calls, they expect you to write a few tickets. Your calls run the gamut. There are what we call 'delayed calls,' a burglary, for example, that occurred a few hours before. You go to bed at night and wake up in the morning to discover your car has been broken into and the radio's gone.

"I work day the day shift from 6:30 in the morning until 2:30 P.M. During that time period we get a lot of delayed calls. The afternoon shift and midnight shift guys get a lot of what we call 'in progress calls.' You'll get up at two o'clock in the morning to go to the bathroom and you'll look out the window and see the light on inside your car.

"But we get silly calls, too. Back when I was working the midnight shift I had someone call me up to tell me that her toilet was overflowing. They don't know who to call so they call the police. I suggest a plumber, but meanwhile, we're obligated to go out there and I reach behind the lady's toilet and shut off the water.

"These kinds of things get repetitive. You do them every day and it gets old. But I'm basically happy doing what I'm doing. I'm working a schedule that's really convenient for my wife and me to take care of our young daughter. I have no real desire to go up the ladder to sergeant, which is the next step. Although it's a raise in pay and status, I'd lose my seniority and have to go back to the midnight shift. Maybe later, once my daughter is in school, that could be an option.

"There are certain types of calls that I like. I do like working traffic accidents. That interests me. And what feels really nice is when someone gives you a hearty thank you for something you've done. If they've broken down along side of the road and you stop and get them a tow truck, for example. They're extremely grateful for the help. And even better than that is when they write to the sheriff to say what a good job they feel you've done. That goes in your file and stays in your file."

How Rick Fitzgerald Got Started

"My father has been a policeman for about 23 years. I went to college and got my bachelor's degree in business from Florida International University. That was in 1985. At that time a million people had business degrees, so I wondered what I would do. The opportunity to become a policeman was there, it had always been in the back of mind, so I decided to pursue it. I went to City Hall and picked up an application. They hired me and put me through training. The police academy program took four months. I started getting a paycheck the minute I entered the academy. The irony was that I made more money during training than when I first came out to do police work. That was because you go to the police academy 10 hours a day, 50 hours a week. You're getting 10 hours of overtime each week. Once you graduate, you don't put in that kind of regular overtime, so your pay drops down."

Expert Advice

"My advice is probably the same thing my father told me: Just go in, do your eight hours and go home. Don't get involved in the politics of the game, don't get involved talking about people behind their back, it will just get you jammed up."

● ● ●

FOR MORE INFORMATION

Information about entrance requirements may be obtained from federal, state, and local civil service commissions or police departments.

Contact any Office of Personnel Management Job Information Center for pamphlets providing general information and instructions for submitting an application for jobs as Treasury special agents, drug enforcement agents, FBI special agents, or U.S. marshals. Look under "U.S. Government, Office of Personnel Management," in your telephone directory to obtain a local telephone number.

Information about law enforcement careers in general may be obtained from:

International Union of Police Associations
1016 Duke Street
Alexandria, VA 22314

CHAPTER 3 Aviation

EDUCATION
H.S. Required
B.A./B.S. Recommended
Other

$$$ SALARY/EARNINGS
$40,000 to $75,000+

OVERVIEW

Aircraft Pilots

Pilots are highly trained professionals who fly airplanes and helicopters to carry out a wide variety of tasks. Although most pilots transport passengers and cargo, others are involved in more unusual tasks, such as dusting crops, spreading seed for reforestation, testing aircraft, directing firefighting efforts, tracking criminals, monitoring traffic, and rescuing and evacuating injured persons. The vast majority of pilots fly airplanes.

Except on small aircraft, the cockpit crew usually consists of two pilots. Generally, the most experienced pilot (the captain) is in command and supervises all other crew members. The copilot assists in communicating with air traffic controllers, monitoring the instruments, and flying the aircraft. Some large aircraft still have a third pilot–the flight engineer–in the cockpit who assists the other pilots by monitoring and operating many of the instruments and systems, making minor inflight repairs, and watching for other aircraft. New technology can perform many flight tasks, however, and virtually all new aircraft now fly with only two pilots, who rely more heavily on computerized controls.

Before departure, pilots plan their flights carefully. They thoroughly check their aircraft to make sure that the engines, controls, instruments, and other systems are functioning properly.

They also make sure that the baggage or cargo has been loaded correctly. They confer with flight dispatchers and aviation weather forecasters to find out about weather conditions en route and at their destination. Based on this information, they choose a route, altitude, and speed that should provide the fastest, safest, and smoothest flight. When flying under instrument flight rules (those procedures governing the operation of the aircraft when there is poor visibility), the pilot in command or the company dispatcher usually files an instrument flight plan with air traffic control, so that the flight can be coordinated with other air traffic.

Takeoff and landing are the most difficult parts of the flight and require close coordination between the pilot and copilot. For example, as the plane accelerates for takeoff, the pilot concentrates on the runway while the copilot scans the instrument panel. To calculate the speed they must attain to become airborne, pilots consider the altitude of the airport, the outside temperature, the weight of the plane, and the speed and direction of the wind. The moment the plane reaches takeoff speed, the copilot informs the pilot, who then pulls back on the controls to raise the nose of the plane.

Unless the weather is bad, the actual flight is relatively easy. With the assistance of autopilot and the flight management computer, the pilots steer the plane along their planned route. Along the way they are monitored by the air traffic control stations they pass. They continuously scan the instrument panel to check their fuel supply, the condition of their engines, and the air-conditioning, hydraulic, and other systems. Pilots may request a change in altitude or route if the circumstances call for it. For example, if the ride is rougher than expected, they might ask air traffic control if pilots flying at other altitudes have reported better conditions. If so, they may request a change. This procedure also may be used to find a stronger tailwind or a weaker headwind in order to save fuel and increase speed.

Because helicopters are used for short trips at relatively low altitude, helicopter pilots must be constantly on the lookout for trees, bridges, power lines, transmission towers, and other dangerous obstacles. Regardless of the type of aircraft, all pilots must monitor the warning devices designed to help detect sudden shifts in wind conditions, which can cause crashes.

If visibility is poor, pilots must rely completely on their instruments. Using the altimeter readings, they can determine how high above ground they are and whether or not they can fly safely over mountains and other obstacles. Special navigation radios give pilots precise information that, with the help of special maps, tells them their exact position. Other very sophisticated equipment provides directions to a point just above the end of a runway, which enables pilots to land completely blind.

Once on the ground, pilots must complete records on their flight for their organization or company and for the Federal Aviation Administration (FAA).

The number of nonflying duties that pilots have depends on the employment setting. Airline pilots can draw on the services of large support staffs; consequently they perform few nonflying duties. Pilots employed by other organizations, such as charters or business operators, have many other ancillary duties. They may load the aircraft, handle all passenger luggage to ensure a balanced load, and supervise refueling. Other nonflying responsibilities can include keeping records, scheduling flights, arranging for major maintenance, and performing minor maintenance and repair work on their aircraft.

Some pilots work as instructors, teaching their students the principles of flight in ground-school classes and demonstrating how to operate aircraft in dual-controlled planes and helicopters. A few specially trained pilots work as examiners or check pilots. They periodically fly with other pilots or applicants to make sure that they are fully capable.

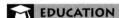 **EDUCATION**
H.S. Required
On-the-Job Training Possible
B.A./B.S. Recommended
Other

$$$ SALARY/EARNINGS
$12,000 to $50,000

Flight Attendants

It is the job of the flight attendant to see that all passengers have a safe, comfortable, and enjoyable flight. At least one hour before each flight, attendants are briefed by the captain on such things as expected weather conditions and special passenger problems. The attendants see that the passenger cabin is in order, that supplies of food, beverages, blankets, and reading material are adequate, and that first aid kits and other emergency equipment are aboard and in working order. As passengers board the plane, attendants greet them, check their tickets, and assist them in storing coats and carry-on luggage.

Before the plane takes off, attendants instruct passengers in the use of emergency equipment and check to see that all passengers have their seat belts fastened and seat backs forward. Once in the air, attendants answer questions about the flight; distribute reading material, pillows, and blankets; and help care for small children, elderly, and disabled persons. They may administer first aid to passengers who become ill. Attendants also serve cocktails and other refreshments and, on many flights, heat and distribute precooked meals. After the plane has landed, flight attendants assist passengers as they leave the plane. They then prepare reports on medications given to passengers, lost and found articles, and cabin equipment conditions. Some flight attendants straighten up the plane's cabin.

Helping passengers in the event of an emergency is the most important responsibility of the flight attendant. This may range from reassuring passengers when the plane encounters strong turbulence to directing passengers in evacuating a plane following an emergency landing.

Lead or first flight attendants aboard planes oversee the work of the other attendants while performing most of the same duties.

EDUCATION
H.S. Required
On-the-Job Training Possible
B.A./B.S. Recommended
Other

$$$ SALARY/EARNINGS
$20,000 to $75,000

Air Traffic Controllers

The air traffic control system is a vast network of people and equipment that ensures the safe operation of commercial and private aircraft. Air traffic controllers coordinate the movement of air traffic to make certain that planes stay a safe distance apart. Their immediate concern is safety, but controllers also must direct planes efficiently to minimize delays. Some controllers regulate airport traffic; others regulate flights between airports.

Although airport tower or terminal controllers keep track of all the planes traveling through the airport's airspace, their main responsibility is to organize the flow of aircraft in and out of the airport. Relying on radar and visual observation, they closely monitor each plane to ensure a safe distance between all aircraft and to guide pilots between the hangar or ramp and the end of the airport's airspace. In addition, controllers keep pilots informed about changes in weather conditions, such as wind shear, a sudden change in the velocity or direction of the wind that can cause the pilot to lose control of the aircraft.

During arrival or departure, several controllers handle each plane. As a plane approaches an airport, the pilot radios ahead to inform the terminal of its presence. The controller in the radar room just beneath the control tower has a copy of the plane's flight plan and already has observed the plane on radar. If the way is clear, the controller directs the pilot to a runway; if the airport is busy, the plane is fitted into a traffic pattern with other aircraft waiting to land. As the plane nears the runway, the pilot is asked to contact the tower. There, another controller, who is also watching the plane on radar, monitors the aircraft for the last mile or so of its approach to the runway, and delays any departures that would interfere with the plane's landing.

Once the plane has landed, a ground controller in the tower directs it along the taxiways to its assigned gate. The ground controller usually works entirely by sight, but may use radar if visibility is very poor.

The procedure is reversed for departures. The ground controller directs the plane to the proper runway. The local controller then informs the pilot about conditions at the airport, such as the weather, speed and direction of wind, and visibility. This controller also issues runway clearance for the pilot to take off. Once in the air, the plane is guided out of the airport's airspace by the departure controller.

After each plane departs, airport tower controllers notify the controllers en route who will next take charge. There are 22 en route control centers located around the country, each employing 300 to 700 controllers, with more than 150 on duty during peak hours at the busier facilities. Airplanes generally fly along designated routes; each center is assigned a certain airspace containing many different routes.

In addition to airport towers and en route centers, air traffic controller specialists also work in flight service stations operated at over 100 locations. These specialists provide pilots with information on the station's particular area, including terrain, preflight and inflight weather information, suggested routes, and other information important to the safety of a flight. Flight service station specialists help pilots in emergency situations and participate in searches for missing or overdue aircraft. However, they are not involved in actively managing air traffic.

TRAINING

Aircraft Pilots

All pilots who are paid to transport passengers or cargo must have a commercial pilot's license with an instrument rating issued by the FAA. Helicopter pilots must hold a commercial pilot's certificate with a helicopter rating. To qualify for these licenses, applicants must be at least 18 years old and have at least 250 hours of flight experience. The time can be reduced through participation in certain school curricula approved by the FAA.

Pilots must pass a strict physical examination to ensure that they are in good health and have 20/20 vision with or without glasses, good hearing, and no physical handicaps that could impair their performance. Applicants must also pass a written test, which includes questions on the principles of safe flight, navigation techniques, and FAA regulations. They also need to demonstrate their flying ability to FAA or designated examiners.

To fly in periods of low visibility, pilots must be rated by the FAA to fly by instruments. Pilots may qualify for this rating by accruing a total of 105 hours of flight experience, including 40 hours of experience in flying by instruments; passing a written examination on procedures and FAA regulations covering instrument flying; and demonstrating their ability to fly by instruments.

Airline pilots must fulfill additional requirements. They must pass FAA written and flight examinations to earn a flight engineer's license. Captains are required to have an airline transport pilot's license. Applicants for this license must be at least 23 years old and have a minimum of 1,500 hours of flying experience, including night and instrument flying.

All licenses remain valid as long as a pilot can pass the periodic physical examinations and tests of flying skills required by government and company regulations.

The armed forces have always been an important source of trained pilots for civilian jobs. Military pilots gain valuable experience on jet aircraft and helicopters, and many organizations prefer pilots with this experience. This is primarily a reflection of the extensive flying time acquired by military pilots. The FAA has certified about 600 civilian flying schools, and some colleges and universities offer degree credit for certified pilot training. In recent years, the armed services have increased financial incentives in an effort to retain more pilots. This has shifted more of the burden for training pilots to FAA certified schools. Over the next several years, the number of available pilots who have been trained in the military should increase, as reductions in military budgets result in more pilots leaving military service. Over the long haul, however, fewer pilots will be trained by the armed forces; this will mean that FAA certified schools will do more of the training.

Although some small airlines will hire high-school graduates, most airlines require two years of college, preferring to hire college graduates. In fact, most entrants to this occupation have a college degree. If the number of college educated applicants increases, employers may raise their educational requirements. Because pilots must be able to make quick decisions and accurate judgments under pressure, airline companies reject applicants who do not pass required psychological and aptitude tests.

New airline pilots usually start as copilots. Although airlines favor applicants who already have a flight engineer's license, they may train those who have only the commercial license. All new pilots receive several weeks of intensive training in simulators and classrooms before being assigned to a flight.

Organizations other than airlines generally require less flying experience. However, a commercial pilot's license is a minimum requirement, and employers prefer applicants who have experience in the type of craft they will be flying. New employees usually start as copilots or flying less sophisticated equipment. Test pilots often are required to have an engineering degree.

Flight Attendants

Airlines prefer to hire poised, tactful, and resourceful people who can deal comfortably with strangers. Applicants usually must be at least 19 to 21 years old, but some airlines have higher minimum age requirements. Flight attendants must fall into a specific weight range depending on their height, and must have excellent health, good vision, and the ability to speak clearly.

Applicants must be high-school graduates. Those having several years of college or experience in dealing with the public are preferred. More and more of the attendants being hired have college degrees. Flight attendants for international airlines generally must speak an appropriate foreign language fluently.

Most large airlines require that newly hired flight attendants complete four to six weeks of intensive training in the airlines' own schools. The airlines that do not operate schools generally send new employees to the school of another airline. Transportation to the training centers and an allowance for board, room, and school supplies may be provided. Trainees learn emergency procedures, such as evacuating an airplane, operating an oxygen system, and giving first aid. Attendants also are taught flight regulations and duties as well as company operations and policies. Trainees might also receive instruction on personal grooming and weight control. Trainees for the international routes get additional instruction in passport and customs regulations and dealing with terrorism. Towards the end of their training, students go on practice flights. Attendants must receive 12 to 14 hours of training in emergency procedures and passenger relations annually.

After completing initial training, flight attendants are assigned to one of their airline's bases. New attendants are placed in reserve status and are called on either to staff extra flights or fill in for attendants who are sick or on vacation. Reserve attendants on duty must be available on short notice. Attendants usually remain on reserve for at least one year; at some cities, it may take five years or longer to advance from reserve to regular status. Advancement takes longer today than in the past, because experienced attendants are remaining in this career for more years than they used to. Attendants who no longer are on reserve bid for regular assignments. Because these assignments are based on seniority, usually only the most experienced attendants get their choice of base and flights.

Some attendants transfer to flight service instructor, customer service director, recruiting representative, or various other administrative positions.

Air Traffic Controllers

Air traffic controller trainees are selected through the competitive Federal Civil Service system. Applicants must pass a written test that measures their ability to learn the controller's duties. Applicants with experience as a pilot, navigator, or military controller can improve their rating by scoring well on the occupational knowledge portion of the examination. Among the aptitudes the exam measures are abstract reasoning and three-dimensional spatial visualization. In addition, applicants generally must have three years of general work experience or four years of college, or a combination of both. Applicants also must survive a one-week screening at the FAA's Aeronautical Center Academy in Oklahoma City, which includes aptitude tests using computer simulators and physical and psychological examinations. Successful applicants receive drug screening tests.

For airport tower and en route center positions, applicants must be less than 31 years old. Older candidates are eligible for positions at flight-service stations.

Controllers must be articulate, because they need to give directions to pilots quickly and clearly. Intelligence and a good memory also are important, as controllers constantly receive information that they must immediately grasp, interpret, and remember. Controllers must also be decisive, because they often have to make quick decisions without hesitating. The ability to concentrate is crucial, as they must make these decisions in the midst of noise and other distractions.

Trainees learn their craft through a combination of formal and on-the-job training. They receive three to four months of intensive training at the FAA academy, where they learn the fundamentals of the airway system, FAA regulations, controller equipment, aircraft performance characteristics, as well as more specialized tasks. Based on aptitude and test scores, trainees are selected to work at either an en route center or a tower. Regardless of the type of training, students must demonstrate their ability to make quick, correct decisions in simulated air traffic situations. After graduation, it takes several years of progressively more responsible work experience, interspersed with considerable classroom instruction and independent study, to become a fully qualified controller. This training includes instruction in the operation of the new, more automated air traffic control system, including the automated Microwave Landing System that enables pilots to receive instructions over automated data links.

At airports, new controllers begin by supplying pilots with basic flight data and airport information. They then advance to ground controller, then local controller, departure controller, and finally, arrival controller. At an en route traffic control center, new controllers first deliver printed flight plans to teams, gradually advancing to radar associate controller and then radar controller.

Failure to become certified in any position at a facility within a specified time may result in dismissal. Controllers who fail to complete either the academy or the on-the-job portion of the training are usually dismissed. Controllers must pass a physical examination each year and a job performance examination twice each year.

JOB OUTLOOK

Pilots

Pilots are expected to face considerable competition for jobs through the year 2005 because the number of applicants for new positions is expected to exceed the number of openings. Aircraft pilots understandably have an extremely strong attachment to their occupation, as it requires a substantial investment in specialized training and can offer very high earnings. In addition, the glamour, prestige, and travel benefits make this a very desirable occupation, and pilots rarely change occupations.

However, because of the large number of pilots who will reach retirement age over the next decade or so, replacement needs will generate several thousand job openings each year.

Additional jobs will be created from rising demand for pilots. Employment is expected to increase faster than the average for all occupations through the year 2005. While computerized flight management systems will all but eliminate the demand for flight engineers, the expected growth in airline passenger and cargo traffic will create a need for more airliners, pilots, and flight instructors. Employment of business pilots is expected to grow more slowly than in the past, as more businesses opt to fly with regional and smaller airlines serving their area rather than buy and maintain their own aircraft. On the other hand, jobs for helicopter pilots are expected to grow more rapidly as their services are increasingly in demand.

Opportunities for aircraft pilots will be poor in the short run, as an increasing number of pilots will leave the armed forces and look for jobs in the civilian sector. This situation will be further compounded by the large number of pilots who have lost their jobs during the restructuring of the airline industry. The mergers and bankruptcies of the past few years have created a glut of trained pilots. As this glut is absorbed over the next few years, prospects should improve dramatically. Pilots who have logged the greatest number of flying hours in the more sophisticated equipment generally have the best prospects. This is the reason military pilots usually have an advantage over other applicants. Job seekers with the most FAA licenses will also have a competitive advantage.

Flight Attendants

As more career-minded people have entered this occupation, turnover, which traditionally has been very high, has declined. Nevertheless, most job openings through the year 2005 should flow from replacement needs. Thousands of job openings will arise each year to replace those flight attendants who transfer to another occupation or leave the labor force.

Employment of flight attendants is expected to grow much faster than the average for all occupations through the year 2005. Growth in population and income is expected to increase the number of airline passengers. Moreover, airlines expand their capacity by increasing the number and size of planes in operation. Since Federal Aviation Administration safety rules require one attendant for every 50 seats, more flight attendants will be needed.

Competition for jobs as flight attendants is expected to remain very keen because the number of applicants is expected to greatly exceed the number of job openings. The glamour of the airline industry and the opportunity to travel and meet people attract many applicants. Candidates with at least two years of college and experience in dealing with the public have the best chance of being hired.

Employment of flight attendants is sensitive to cyclical swings in the economy. During recessions, when the demand for air travel declines, many flight attendants are put on part-time status or laid off. Until demand increases, few new attendants are hired.

Air Traffic Controllers

The FAA reports a hiring freeze for controllers that will be in effect through 1996 and possibly into 1997. Employment of air traffic controllers is expected to grow more slowly than the average for all occupations through the year 2005. Employment growth is not expected to keep pace with growth in the number of aircraft flying, largely due to the introduction of labor-saving air traffic control equipment that should make controllers more productive.

Competition for air traffic controller jobs is expected to remain keen. The occupation attracts many more qualified applicants than the small number of job openings stemming from growth of the occupation and replacement needs. Turnover is very low; because of the relatively high pay and liberal retirement benefits, controllers have a very strong attachment to the occupation.

Because most of the current work force was hired after the controller's strike during the 1980s, the average age of the current work force is still fairly young. As a result, most controllers will not be eligible to retire until 2005 or later.

Air traffic controllers who continue to meet the proficiency and medical requirements enjoy more job security than most workers. The demand for air travel and the workloads of air traffic controllers decline during recessions, but controllers seldom are laid off.

SALARIES

Pilots

Airline pilots are among the highest paid in the nation. According to the Future Aviation Professionals of America, the 1992 average salary for airline pilots was about $80,000 a year; for flight engineers, $42,000; for copilots, $65,000; and for captains, $107,000. Some senior captains on the largest aircraft earned as much as $165,000. Earnings depend on factors such as the type, size, and maximum speed of the plane, and the number of hours and miles flown. Extra pay may be given for night and international flights.

Generally, pilots working outside the airlines earn lower salaries. According to a survey conducted by the National Business Aircraft Association, the median salary for chief pilots was $62,000 a year in 1992; for captains/pilots, $57,900; and for copilots, $42,000. Pilots who fly jet aircraft usually earn higher salaries than nonjet pilots.

Most airline pilots are eligible for life and health insurance plans financed by the airlines. They also receive retirement benefits and, if they fail the FAA physical examination at some point in their careers, they receive disability payments. Some airlines provide allowances to pilots for purchasing and cleaning their uniforms. As an additional benefit, pilots and their immediate families usually are entitled to free or reduced-fare transportation on their own and other airlines.

Most airline pilots are members of the Airline Pilots Association, International. Those employed by one major airline are members of the Allied Pilots Association. Some flight engineers are members of the Flight Engineers' International Association.

Flight Attendants

Beginning flight attendants had median earnings of about $13,000 a year in 1992, according to data from the Association of Flight Attendants. Flight attendants with six years of flying experience had median annual earnings of about $20,000; some senior flight attendants earned as much as $40,000 a year. Flight attendants receive extra compensation for overtime and for night and international flights. In addition, flight attendants and their immediate families are entitled to reduced fares on their own and most other airlines.

Many flight attendants belong to the Association of Flight Attendants. Others are members of the Transport Workers Union of America, The International Brotherhood of Teamsters, or other unions.

Flight attendants are required to buy uniforms and wear them while on duty. Uniform replacement items are usually paid for by the company. The airlines generally provide a small allowance to cover cleaning and upkeep of the uniforms.

Air Traffic Controllers

Air traffic controllers in training programs in 1995 earned $24,038 a year. After graduation and on the first assignment, salaries for new air traffic controllers began at about $29,000. Raises and cost of living increases come every year.

Controllers at the grade 9 level and above earn 5 percent more than other federal workers in an equivalent grade. A controller's pay is determined by both the worker's job responsibilities and the complexity of the particular facility. Earnings are higher at those facilities where traffic patterns are more complex. In 1995 controllers averaged over $55,800 a year.

Depending on length of service, controllers receive 13 to 26 days of paid vacation and 13 days of paid sick leave each year, as well as life insurance and health benefits. In addition, controllers can retire at an earlier age and with fewer years of service than other federal employees. Air traffic controllers are eligible to retire at age 50 with 20 years of service as an active air traffic controller, or after 25 years of active service at any age. There is a mandatory retirement age of 56 for controllers who manage air traffic.

RELATED FIELDS

Pilots

Although they are not in the cockpit, air traffic controllers and dispatchers also play an important role in making sure flights are safe and on schedule, and participate in many of the decisions pilots must make.

Flight Attendants

Other jobs that involve helping people as a safety professional and require the ability to be pleasant even under trying circumstances include emergency medical technician, firefighter, and maritime crew.

Air Traffic Controllers

Other occupations that involve the direction and control of traffic in air transportation are airline-radio operator and airplane dispatcher.

INTERVIEW
Jim Carr
Pilot

Jim Carr has been flying since 1967. He is a Boeing 757 captain with America West. He got his commercial license when he was in the Air Force and has been flying commercially since 1980. In 1971 he earned his B.S. in Aerospace Engineering and Mechanics from the University of Minnesota in Minneapolis.

What the Job's Really Like

"Typical to a day's work is checking in about an hour prior to departure time. We go to our dispatch center, which has a lot of computers and individuals who plan all the flights, monitor the weather, and all those sorts of things. They provide us with a flight plan–the route of flight that we have filed with the air traffic controllers. We sign off on that, then we proceed to the airplane and do a series of preflight checks. These include verifying the maintenance data, a preflight inspection of both the exterior of the plane–we're looking for any apparent damage or anything that looks abnormal, leaks, that sort of thing–then a cockpit check before we leave the gate.

"Most modern turbojet airliners now have two pilots–a captain and a first officer. We do our checks, then we go over a formal checklist to ensure all the switches and controls are in the proper position before we leave the gate.

"There's activity galore during that process. The fuelers are fueling the plane, the flight attendants are doing their own safety checks, then we start boarding passengers. There's just a lot of activity as we get closer and closer to the push back time, our published departure time. The push back is when we back off from the gate.

"We taxi out to an assigned runway and are cleared for take off and away we go. It's a matter of flying the airplane and accomplishing the procedures set by the FAA–99.9 percent of the flights are routine. When something happens, we analyze the situation and take whatever appropriate action is necessary. I've never had what I'd call a close call. I've had hydraulic systems fail and an engine quit, but we're trained to handle that. An airplane can fly quite well with only one engine operating. It's really a testament to the equipment we're flying these days. There are so many backup systems, rarely, rarely, do you ever have a serious problem.

"On top of that every six months we're back in the simulator practicing. In a two-hour simulator session a pilot can experience more emergencies than he or she would ever experience in a career.

"Landing is one of the most fun parts. I think most pilots enjoy that the most. You're actually manipulating the aircraft controls with your hands and feet, as opposed to letting the autopilot fly. Flying is really just a series of correcting for the last mistake that was made. That's not a negative statement. Flying an aircraft in our atmosphere is just a real dynamic situation and so you're constantly making corrections to get the airplane from point *A* to point *B*.

"Once we land, the work isn't over. We have to find our way to the gate. Sometimes that can be more difficult than finding the airport from the air. There are many more dangers on the ground than are in the air. All the vehicles and people–you have to keep your eyes peeled.

"We have a shut–down checklist, then we fill out the maintenance log, then I'm cleared to leave. If I'm back at my domicile, I head home. If I'm on the road we gather up the crew and go out to the curb and take a shuttle to the hotel where we spend our layover. That can be anywhere from 9 to 24 hours. The purpose of the layover is to rest up for your next flight.

"The downside is that you have to spend extended periods away from your family. Most airline pilots will fly anywhere from 60 to 85 hours a month, which doesn't sound like a lot if you compare it with a 40- or 50-hour work week. But to get that 60 to 85 hours of flight time, you're on duty for upwards of 300 hours a month.

"A lot of people who don't do much traveling really like to stay in a hotel once in a while. It's a nice change of pace. You don't have to make your bed yourself and all that sort of stuff. But after a while they all start looking pretty much the same. It seems that you spend an awful lot of time in hotels, just waiting for the airplane to come back so you can leave. You can use that time to read and do other things, but it still seems like endless periods of time.

"And during a long flight, you have to fight boredom and fatigue. You take a break, get up and walk around, talk with your copilot.

"My routes vary from month to month. That's typical of most airlines. The pilots are given flight schedules based on their seniority and their choice of published schedules for the coming month. My schedule over the last few months has been flying from Phoenix to Chicago and Phoenix to Newark or New York City.

"It's not so much the preference of the airport or the route. It provides the specific days off I need for personal business. Unlike a professional who works in an office, if I need to take the car in to the garage I can't just say I'll be in late. When I have a flight leaving I can't take the car in. You have to plan those types of things a little bit further in advance. Usually I fly three or four days a week. Typically, it will be a three-day trip. You leave home, you're gone for two nights, and you're back on the third. You might come in and fly another one or two day trip during the week. But I can choose my days off more or less. And the time off away from duty is yours.

"I love the flying part most of all–to be up in the sky and to be able to look at the wonders of nature. You can see thunderstorms and weather fronts and wind storms on the ground– all kinds of things, the leaves changing. It's certainly a view of the world not everyone gets to see, at least not with the frequency we do.

"The upsides are the potential for a very nice income. Most starting salaries are about $30,000, then it goes up to $45,000 to $50,000 by the second year. The big jump is when you become a captain and move over to the left seat. Twelve years into the company, captains at America West are making about $115,000 a year. At other airlines, flying similar aircraft, pilots are making $150,000 to $180,000.

"Generally, we work under the seniority system. All promotions and upward movement depend upon when you were hired. So, if you were to switch airlines, you'd be starting from the bottom again.

"I'm kind of biased, but I think it's the greatest job in the world. Most pilots feel real fortunate that we do a job we really enjoy doing. And while I look forward to having time off, at the end of my three or four days off I'm always looking forward to going back to work. Not many people in the workforce have that same feeling."

How Jim Carr Got Started

"As far back as I can remember I was fascinated with airplanes. As a little kid I had a strong interest there. While I was on a summer job between high school and college, a friend brought in a five-dollar coupon for an introductory offer to fly your first lesson. It was just awesome. That gave me the bug and I continued after that and got my private license. I flew a little bit through college and once I graduated from college I went into the U.S. Air Force and stayed there for 10 years.

"I first started flying for Air Florida. That was in 1980. After two years I moved to Phoenix where I am now, with America West. I started out as a line pilot and was asked to join the management group in 1985. I became the assistant chief pilot and ultimately the chief pilot. Then in 1987 I became Vice President of Flight Operations. I stayed with that until February of 1995. All through my administrative tenure I continued to fly. Now I fly full-time."

Expert Advice

"I would advise you to work real hard in school and get as good a background in mathematics and science as you possibly can. The more modern the aircraft cockpits and systems become, the more that type of a science/engineering/mathematics background really helps to understand how all of it works. We don't have to build the airplanes, but situations come up and a deeper understanding really helps in troubleshooting problems.

"Another thing is that you have to be really conscious of your health and adopt a healthy lifestyle."

INTERVIEW

Gracie Anderson
Flight Attendant

Gracie has been a flight attendant for 12 years.

What the Job's Really Like

"The work is exhausting–you're on your feet a lot, you have very strange hours. And the time differences really affect you. I fly to

Chicago and Newark and my overnights are in San Diego. But I have a lot of other choices, too. We fly coast-to-coast and all points in between.

"We look at ourselves as the most important safety feature on the aircraft. That's because of our knowledge of how to get out and what to do. But a lot of the passengers are only thinking about getting their drinks. If they don't get it as soon as they want it, they think their lives are over. They don't look at us as the person who will save them if anything should happen.

"Our primary role is safety; secondary is service. But being in the transportation business, you really have to play up the service part of it.

"During takeoff we're very busy. Probably the most exhausting part of the flight is just getting everybody on. I try to remember that, when I have 100 plus people on my flight, they're not all on vacation. Some are going for work, some have just lost somebody near to them. Or they just lost the biggest deal of their life or they're going to present the biggest deal of their life. And they're all sitting in this tiny little tube together and the emotions are just running the gamut.

"Add the fear of flying to that–well, it's not routine for all of them, there is stress and a lot of nerves.

"Dealing with the passengers can be the hardest part. Recently, on a flight, even before we left, I had a passenger who was back in the bathroom smoking. One of the other flight attendants said something to her about it, but she denied it. Later on, we were really delayed, and as we got closer to Phoenix she came back to ask for something to drink and I could smell the cigarette smoke. I understand the addiction because I used to smoke, but it's not so much that they snuck a cigarette, it's the fact that they lied to me and I don't know where they put their cigarette. That's where our biggest fear comes from, that something will cause a fire. I put on gloves and went through the trash can in the rest room. This is where the glamour comes in. It was really disgusting. I found the butt in the trash can along with nothing but paper.

"We have to serve the food. We turn the ovens on and heat up the food, then place the trays in the cart to pass out. But passengers can get so impatient. It's not as if we can stand up right after takeoff. We have headsets to pass out, too, if there's a movie and someone else is passing out the drinks. And in the middle of all of this, there's always a passenger asking, 'Can I have a pillow? Can I change seats? What about my connection?' It's constant questions. And that's why sometimes passing out the food or drinks takes longer. We're constantly getting interrupted. But, then that's what we're there for.

"It's easy to feel harried. It's not like you are out of control or anything, but sometimes you wish they'd just give you five minutes.

"And it's easy to feel unappreciated. I've been talked to horribly. The majority of people I deal with are really very nice, but you always have that handful. And you have to realize they're like that to everyone. You just have to keep your sense of humor. And it always feels really good to get home.

"At the beginning the travel part was great. I was single and you'd go out and have fun in different cities. But as time wore on that kind of got old. Now I'm married and I have twin daughters. Sometimes my husband comes with me on my overnight flights, which is fun. But my objective is different now. Get there, do my trip, and come home.

"The time off is unbelievable. I can't beat it. I get about 19 days off a month, so I get to see my kids more than most people. I've gotten to see more of the world than I ever thought I would. Although we don't go there anymore, America West used to fly overseas. I've flown to Nagoya, Japan, for example. I might not have picked it as a vacation spot, but still I got to see it and had my hotel paid for–it was great. I've been to Hawaii I don't know how many times, and also just around the states. It's been unbelievable. Plus, you get more or less free flights when you're not working. You also get car rental and hotel discounts.

"Salaries are another downside, though. It's not like what it used to be. The older attendants make anywhere from $40,000 to $60,000. But the airline started what they call a "B" scale for the new hirees. They start off somewhere around $12,000 or $13,000 a year.

"Sometimes I sit there and I think, 'What are we doing? We're a flying restaurant sailing through the sky with a hundred thousand pounds of fuel under us. Who in their right mind is going to get into this thing?'

"But most of the people are really, really wonderful. You'll have someone come up to you and say that's it's been the best flight they ever had and that makes up for everything."

How Gracie Anderson Got Started

"I did this on a bet. Back in 1985 my brother-in-law told me that America West was hiring, so I called them up. They put me through three or four interviews and that's how I ended up getting the job. The first interview was a group interview with about 30 other applicants. You had to get up and talk about yourself and say what you were doing at that time. Then it went to a smaller group interview and they gave you little assignments to do. 'What if such and such happened, what would you do?' That sort of thing. Then it went to a one-on-one interview.

"When I was hired at America West, we were what they called 'cross-utilized.' That meant that not only were we flight attendants, we also worked reservations, the ticket counter at the gate, and down at the ramp. You were never just flying. Three days a week I'd fly, the other days I'd be at the gate or whatever.

"I also went into the training department for a while and taught reservation clerks. I fly full-time now, as cross-utilizations became defunct in 1989 or 90. But every once in a while I still go off the line and do in-flight training for attendants.

"When I started my own training, the program was three months long, because we had to learn everything. Now, for flight attendants it's just three weeks long."

Expert Advice

"I think if you're young and have a lot of energy, it's wonderful. I always joke around and say I'm donning my rhino skin. You need thick skin to do this. I have a flight buddy who teases me and says I'm like Mary Poppins out there. That's what I'm here for. I'm not here to make these people have a miserable trip. I have a hard time saying "no" to them. It has to be something outlandish. I try not to get bothered by petty things. You're going to see a lot of pettiness, but you can't let it get to you. I had a gentleman who had won a lot of stuffed animals. They were all packed away in the overhead bin. Then another passenger comes in and opens up the bin. All of a sudden he starts throwing all these animals. I looked over and I saw a giraffe flying through the cabin, then an elephant and a monkey. He thinks it's his bin because it's over his seat. So sometimes you have to go up to them and say, "No, it's my bin and I'm sharing it with everyone." Sometimes you have to treat them as if they're first-graders. I know it sounds silly, but I try to give people little Life Lessons. If someone doesn't say "please" to me, if they just say, 'Hey, gimme a Coke,' I smile and say, 'What's the magic word?' I do it with a smile. I've been able to say things to people and get away with it, but you have to be able to wear that smile.

"The key to success in this industry is that you have to be extremely flexible. Stuff happens all the time. You get canceled, delayed, diverted–and you have to be able to go with the flow.

"And you can't be chasing the almighty dollar to work at this job. You have to want just time off and flight benefits. That's really where the fun is. I love it. Where else could you put in so little time and have such good benefits?"

INTERVIEW

Karen Seals
Air Traffic Controller

As an air traffic controller, Karen Seals is employed by the Federal Aviation Administration (FAA). She is assigned to Phoenix Airport, but is currently on temporary assignment at Goodyear, a small airport just to the west of Phoenix.

What the Job's Really Like

"I'm responsible for the safety and the efficient flow of traffic. I sequence the airplanes into the airport for landings and takeoffs.

"We work eight hours at a time, five days a week, but we do shift work. At Phoenix we're open seven days a week, 24-hours a day. At Goodyear we're open from six in the morning until nine at night. It depends on the airport. Hours can vary from week to week.

"There is stress involved with this job, but I think the stress varies from person to person. And sometimes people don't even realize what it is that causes the stress. It could be the rotating shifts, with night shifts and coming back early the next morning. That's hard to do. The interruption in your sleeping pattern can cause stress. The actual amount of air traffic can also cause stress.

"For me the most stress comes in when you really have to work together as a team. You have to interact so much, you don't work independently at all–it's all team work. And sometimes when you work with other people there can be conflicts. It's not conflicts of personality, it's just arises because communicating can be difficult. At a bigger airport you could have from nine to twelve controllers working together. At a small airport you work more independently; most of the time there are two on duty together.

"You only have one air space and you have to split it in half, so you constantly have to do something in another controller's air space. In order to do something in that air space you have to get his or her permission. So you are constantly having to communicate and plan ahead.

"We get enough breaks during the day so that you don't get too worn out. You might work for an hour, have a break, then go back to work at a different position where you're doing something entirely different. You divide your time between ground control, where you're taxiing planes to and from the runway, and local control, where you clear them for takeoff and landings. And there are several other positions, too. You get a lot of variety so you don't get tired.

"On the plus side, we get great benefits and time off. We also get to take familiarization trips. They're for training purposes, but you can go on any airline that participates in the program and ride up in the cockpit. And you can go to whatever destination you choose. They have you do this so you can ask questions and learn what it's like in the cockpit. And you do a little liaison work, too.

"It's an exciting job. I'm always happy to go to work. I love what I do. I love to work the airplanes. You put a plan together and ask everybody to do certain things. And everybody actually does what you asked and it works out great. You're getting the airplanes out on time and you're getting them in without problems.

"Because of the way Phoenix is set up–we only have two runways–it's exciting because you're constantly having to plan. If Plan A doesn't work out, you have to have a Plan B. We run a lot of traffic on two runways. We're always busy, always pumped up. There's always something going on. We deal with just over 100 to 120 takeoffs and landings an hour.

"You also get to work in the aviation community, which is a really neat group of people. You get to see all the aspects. You get to work with the pilots, the people down on the ramp, with the airport people and the administrative people. It's such a variety of people and everyone has to depend on each other and help each other out. It's a unique experience."

How Karen Seals Got Started

"I have always loved flying and airplanes. My father is a pilot and we were able to fly quite a bit as kids. That's where my initial exposure came from.

"I was previously employed as a geologist in the 1980s, but it was in one of the down cycles and continued to stay in a down cycle. I kept getting laid off or needed to find a different job. So, since I'd always had a love for aviation, I decided it was time to get out of geology and get some different training so I could work at something more stable.

"I studied at the University of Colorado in Boulder and graduated in 1984 with a B.A. in geology. In 1986 I just opened the phone book and started making calls to the different airports until I finally got the right number for a regional office of the FAA. I asked them how I could become an air traffic controller and they told me that I needed to sign up to take a test. It was an aptitude test with different portions to it. You had to have a fairly high score. I took the test, then ended up waiting a year and a half before they called me. There was a backlog then. While I was waiting, I didn't really think I would hear from them. There had been no contact at all in that year and a half. Then I got a phone call out of the blue. They said they had a date available at the academy in Oklahoma City. It happened to be coming up in the next week. I packed up and went out there. The course took four months.

"During the training I stayed in an apartment set up specifically to accommodate the FAA. We were paid a salary and a per diem during the training period. After I graduated, I started off at Deer Valley Airport on the north side of Phoenix. Then I moved to Phoenix Airport."

Expert Advice

"Hang in there for a couple of years until the hiring starts back up. And if I were just getting out of high school and wanted to pursue this field, I would pick a school where you could get some kind of aviation training, specifically in air traffic. It's more competitive now and, though a college degree isn't necessary, the more training you have the better your chances will be."

• • •

FOR MORE INFORMATION

Pilots

Information about job opportunities in a particular airline and the qualifications required may be obtained by writing to the personnel manager of the airline. For addresses of airline companies and information about job opportunities and salaries, contact:

Future Aviation Professionals of America
4291 J. Memorial Drive
Atlanta, GA 30032

(This organization may be called toll free at 1-800-JET-JOBS.)

For information on airline pilots, contact:

Airline Pilots Association
1625 Massachusetts Avenue, N.W.
Washington, DC 20036

Air Transport Association of America
1709 New York Avenue, N.W.
Washington, DC 20006

For information on helicopter pilots, contact:

Helicopter Association International
1619 Duke Street
Alexandria, VA 22314

For a copy of List of Certificated Pilot Schools, write to:

Superintendent of Documents
U.S. Government Printing Office
Washington, DC 20402

For information about job opportunities in companies other than airlines, consult the classified section of aviation trade magazines and apply to companies that operate aircraft at local airports.

Flight Attendants

Information about job opportunities in a particular airline and the qualifications required may be obtained by writing to the personnel manager of the company. For addresses of airline companies and information about job opportunities and salaries, contact:

> Future Aviation Professionals of America
> 4959 Massachusetts Boulevard
> Atlanta, GA 30337

(This organization may be called toll free at 1-800-Jet-Jobs.)

Air Traffic Controllers

A pamphlet providing general information about controllers and instructions for submitting an application is available from any U.S. Office of Personnel Management Job Information Center. Look under "U.S. Government, Office of Personnel Management" in your telephone book to obtain a local Job Information Center telephone number, and call for a copy of the Air Traffic Controller Announcement. If there is no listing in your telephone book, dial the toll-free number 1-800-555-1212 and request the number of the Office of Personnel Management Job Information Center for your location.

CHAPTER 4 Travel Agents

🎓 EDUCATION
H.S. Required
On-the-Job Training Possible
A.A./A.S. Recommended

$$$ SALARY/EARNINGS
$12,000 to $30,000

OVERVIEW

Of all the industries worldwide, travel and tourism continue to grow at an astounding rate. In fact, according to the Travel Works for America Council, the travel industry is the second largest employer in the United States (the first being health services). Nearly everyone tries to take at least one vacation every year and many people travel frequently on business. Some travel for education or for that special honeymoon or anniversary trip.

At one time or another, most travelers seek out the services of a travel agent to help with all the details of a trip. This means that jobs for travel agents will continue to grow. Travel agents learn about all the different destinations, modes of transportation, hotels, resorts and cruises, then work to match their customers' needs with the services travel providers offer.

Travel agents generally work in an office and deal with customers in person or over the phone. They plot itineraries, make airline and hotel reservations, book passage on cruise ships, or arrange for car rentals.

But first of all, they listen to the needs of their customers and try to develop the best package for each person. They work with affluent, sophisticated travelers and first-timers, such as students trying to save money and travel on a budget. They can book a simple, round-trip air ticket for a person traveling alone, or handle arrangements for hundreds of people traveling to attend a convention or conference.

Some travel agents are generalists; they handle any or all situations. Others specialize in a particular area, such as cruise ships or corporate travel.

Travel agents gather information from different sources. They use computer data bases, attend trade shows, and read trade magazines. They also visit resorts or locations to get first-hand knowledge about a destination.

Travel agents need to keep up with rapidly changing fares and rates, and they have to know who offers the best packages and service. Their most important concern is the satisfaction of their client.

Most travel agents are offered "fam" trips to help familiarize them with a particular cruise line, safari adventure, exclusive resort, or ecological tour. These trips are offered free to the travel agent so they can "test-drive" a destination before suggesting it to their customers. Travel providers understand that a travel agent is more likely to sell what he or she knows and has enjoyed. Travel agents also receive discounted travel on other business trips, as well as on their own vacations.

The downside, however, according to many travel agents, is that they seldom have enough free time to do all the traveling they would like. They are often tied to their desks, especially during peak travel periods in the summer or over important busy holidays.

And the work can be frustrating at times. Customers might not always know what they want, or their plans can change. As a result, the travel agent might have to cancel or reroute destinations that had already been set.

TRAINING

A four-year college degree is not necessary to become a travel agent. It can be helpful, however, and shows commitment and discipline. Most travel agents study for at least two years and earn an associate's degree. Many community colleges and trade and vocational schools offer good programs in travel and tourism or hospitality management.

Some travel agencies are willing to hire inexperienced applicants and provide them with their own training.

For a list of schools offering certified programs, you can write to the American Society of Travel Agents or the Institute of Certified Travel Agents. (Their addresses are listed at the end of this chapter.)

JOB OUTLOOK

Employment of travel agents is expected to grow much faster than the average for all occupations through the year 2005. Many job openings will arise as new agencies open and existing agencies expand, but most will occur as experienced agents transfer to other occupations or leave the labor force.

Spending on travel is expected to increase significantly through the year 2005. As business activity expands, so will business-related travel. Employment of managerial, professional specialty, and sales representative occupations–those who do most business travel–is projected to grow rapidly.

Also, with rising incomes, more people are expected to travel on vacation and to do so more frequently than in the past. In fact, many people take more than one vacation a year.

Charter flights and larger, more efficient planes have brought air transportation within the budgets of more people. So has the easing of government regulation of air fares and routes, which has fostered greater competition among airlines to offer better and more affordable service. In addition, U.S. travel agents organize tours for the growing number of foreign visitors. Although most travel agencies now have automated reservation systems, this has not weakened demand for travel agents.

The travel industry generally is sensitive to economic downturns and political crises, when travel plans are likely to be deferred. Therefore, the number of job opportunities fluctuates.

SALARIES

Salaries vary according to the region in which you work and your experience. Depending on the agency, you could start out on an hourly wage or receive a yearly salary. Some travel agents prefer to work on a commission basis. That way, the more trips they sell, the more money they earn. A salary plus commission is usually the best combination for travel agents.

Travel agents who are good salespeople can also earn bonuses or more free or discounted trips. If your pay is initially low, it can be offset by this added benefit.

RELATED FIELDS

Other workers with similar duties include secretaries, tour guides, airline reservation agents, and rental car agents.

INTERVIEW
Vivan Portela Buscher
Travel Agent

Vivian Portela Buscher started out as a ticket agent and in passenger services for the airlines, then moved to a wellknown cruise line as a booking agent. It was a natural progression for her to become a travel agent specializing in cruise travel. She has now worked for the same agency since 1987.

What the Job's Really Like

"I work Monday through Friday, and because our agency is open from 9:00 A.M. to 9:00 P.M., I get to choose my hours during the day. Most people prefer to work earlier hours, but I don't. I work from 10:30 A.M. to 7:00 P.M.

"Basically, what I do is this: people who have an interest in taking a cruise vacation call me, and I find them the right cruise at the right price. I think of it more as a matching game rather than a selling situation. My office doesn't call anyone asking them to buy a cruise–everyone calls us.

"I enjoy travel a lot and it's nice to be able to talk about it all day long and to help people find the right travel experience. There's a lot of satisfaction when someone calls me back and tells me that the cruise was exactly as I had described it and that it was the best vacation of his or her life.

"You also get to travel yourself, to sample all the cruises and be more informed on them. I've been to St. Thomas, San Juan, Nassau, Grand Caymen, Jamaica, St. Lucia, and St. Martin, to name just a few.

"We also get to attend a lot of luncheons and dinners and other inaugural activities to view the new ships.

"It's an office with a very high call volume. And there is always a lot of new information to learn, a lot of intensive studying you have to do to acquire all the product knowledge about all the different cruise lines and packages."

How Vivian Portela Buscher Got Started

"It's easy for me to advise other people about travel because it's something I like to do. I specifically chose to be a travel agent because working with the airlines had been becoming difficult. You had to wait a long time to gain seniority and to have a comfortable work schedule with Saturdays and Sundays off. Plus, with so many airlines going out of business, there are a lot of unemployed people in the industry. The airline I worked for folded 10 years ago and I was happy to switch. I was looking for a job that would still be in the travel industry but that would be more secure and with normal hours.

"When I went to college I studied air carrier management and received a bachelor's degree in transportation management. My experience with the airlines and then with a cruise line also was important in preparing me. The rest I picked up through on-the-job training."

Expert Advice

"It's important to go to college and to get as much training as you can, and then to apply to work for an agency where you can get experience. Even if you get experience without going to school, it's very competitive. Sometimes the person with the most education will get the job over someone with equal experience."

INTERVIEW

Mary Fallon Miller
Travel Agent

Mary Fallon Miller began her career as a travel agent in 1986 when she opened her own agency. In partnership with a relative, she first focused on bus tours, transporting groups to see special events in her area. She later moved on to specialize in cruise travel.

What the Job's Really Like

"When you're just starting out, you're tied to the office and the computer a lot, but a newcomer would get to take at least one week a year, more once you've gained some seniority. The owners of a travel agency get to go on more 'fam' trips, but if someone just starting out is seen as a productive member of the business, he or she would get more opportunities. You'll be sent on the 'Cruise-a-Thon' or to the ski shows, and then you'll become your agency's representative.

"Beginners would probably start working side-by-side with someone more experienced in the agency. They might be placed in a specific department, handling, for example, European travel, cruises, or car rental and air fares. Much of their time will be spent coordinating and arranging details.

"It can be tricky keeping all the details accurate and being able to deal with what we call 'grumps and whiners.' There are people who get very nervous about their travel arrangements and they can complain and make your life miserable. But you have to be able to be compassionate—find out *why* they're so concerned. Maybe they had a bad experience in the past. You have to try to discover as much about your client as possible.

"And there are times when things go wrong. There could be a snow-in at an airport and people miss their connections, or someone in the family dies and they have to cancel their whole cruise reservation at the last minute. You have to be professional and flexible and you have to be on the ball all the time.

"It's a demanding job, but it's satisfying. People come back and say, 'I can't believe you knew exactly what I wanted. That's the best vacation I've ever had. And I'm telling all my friends.' You start getting more and more customers coming in and they ask for you by name. That feels really good. You're making a dream come true, and in a way, that's what you're doing–selling dreams."

How Mary Fallon Miller Got Started

"At the age of seven I sailed across the Atlantic on the S.S. France, and then, later, as a young woman, I accompanied my mother throughout Europe and South America. I fell in love with the glamour and excitement of travel. It gets in your blood; I have a real fascination for other cultures and languages. I realized that a career as a travel agent would allow me to pursue my dream to see more of the world."

Expert Advice

"Read *Time, Newsweek,* and your local newspaper. Try to stay in touch with the world. Listen to National Public Radio or watch the travel channel on television.

"Don't be afraid of learning the computer, study languages and, if you have the chance, participate in a language club or take advantage of a foreign exchange program. I lived in Poland for a summer.

"Most important, learn communication skills. And at the beginning, when you're doing some of the drudgery work, it helps to remember that down the road you will receive discounts and free travel, that you have something you are working toward. The hard work will pay off."

• • •

FOR MORE INFORMATION

American Society of Travel Agents
1101 King Street
Alexandria, VA 22314

Association of Retail Travel Agents
1745 Jefferson Davis Highway, Suite 300
Arlington, VA 22202

Institute of Certified Travel Agents
148 Linden Street
P.O. Box 56
Wellesley, MA 02181

CHAPTER 5 Personal Services

OVERVIEW

Beauty and physical fitness has been a concern for a large portion of the population over the last three decades or so. Acquiring the right look has never been easy; it can require that perfect hairstyle, exquisite nails, a neatly trimmed beard, or just the right make-up–as well as the best, fine-tuned body you can drum into shape.

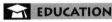
EDUCATION
Other

$$$ SALARY/EARNINGS
$20,000 to $30,000

Barbers and Cosmetologists

As people increasingly demand styles that are better suited to their individual characteristics, they are relying more and more on barbers and cosmetologists. Although tastes and fashions change from year to year, the basic job of barbers and cosmetologists remains the same: to help people look their best.

BARBERS cut, trim, shampoo, and style hair. Many people still go to a barber for just a haircut, but an increasing number seek more personalized hairstyling services. Barbers trained in these areas work in barber shops and styling salons, many of which are considered to be unisex as they serve both men and women. It is not uncommon for a barber to color or perm a customer's hair. In addition, barbers may fit hairpieces, provide hair and scalp treatments, shave male customers, or give facial massages. In most states, barbers are licensed to perform all the duties of cosmetologists except skin care and nail treatment.

COSMETOLOGISTS (OR HAIR STYLISTS) primarily shampoo, cut, and style hair. They also may advise patrons on how to care for their hair. Frequently, they straighten or permanent wave a customer's hair to keep the style in shape. Cosmetologists may also lighten or darken hair color.

In addition, most cosmetologists are trained to give manicures and scalp and facial treatments, provide makeup analysis for women, and clean and style wigs and hairpieces.

Related workers include manicurists, who clean, shape, and polish a customer's fingernails and toenails; makeup artists, who apply makeup; electrologists, who remove hair from skin by electrolysis; and estheticians, who cleanse and beautify the skin. Cosmetologists offer all of the services that barbers do, except shaving men.

 **EDUCATION**
Other

$$$ SALARY/EARNINGS
$20,000 to $50,000

Personal Trainers

Personal trainers work in health clubs, spas, and gyms or in their own private practice. Their work is, in many ways, similar to that of the physical therapist, (see *On the Job: Real People Working in Health Care*) although personal trainers tend to work with a more athletic, healthier population.

TRAINING

Barbers and Cosmetologists

Although all states require barbers and cosmetologists to be licensed, the qualifications necessary to obtain a license vary. Generally, a person must have graduated from a state-licensed barber or cosmetology school, pass a physical examination, and be at least 16 years old. In addition, education requirements vary from state to state–some states require graduation from high school, while others require as little as an eighth grade education. In a few states, completion of an apprenticeship can substitute for graduation from a school, but very few barbers or cosmetologists learn their skills in this way. Applicants for a license usually are required to pass a written test and demonstrate an ability to perform basic barbering or cosmetology services.

Some states have reciprocity agreements that allow licensed barbers and cosmetologists to practice in a different state without additional formal training. Other states do not recognize training or licenses obtained in another state; consequently, persons who wish to become a barber or a cosmetologist should review the laws of the state in which they want to work before entering a training program.

Public and private vocational schools offer daytime or evening classes in barbering and cosmetology. These programs usually last six to twelve months. An apprenticeship program can last from one to two years.

Formal training programs include classroom study, demonstrations, and practical work. Students study the basic services haircutting, shaving, facial massaging, and hair and scalp treatments and, under supervision, practice on customers in school clinics. Most schools also teach unisex hairstyling and chemical styling. Students attend lectures on barber services, the use and care of instruments, sanitation and hygiene, and recognition of certain skin ailments.

Instruction also is given in selling and general business practices. There are advanced courses for experienced barbers in hairstyling, coloring, and the sale and service of hairpieces. Most schools teach hairstyling of men's as well as women's hair.

After graduating from a training program, students can take the state licensing examination. The examination consists of a written test and, in some cases, a practical test of cosmetology skills. A few states include an oral examination in which the applicant is asked to explain the procedures he or she is following while taking the practical test. In some states, a separate examination is given for persons who want only a manicurist license or a facial care license.

Many schools help their graduates find jobs. During their first months on the job, new workers are given relatively simple tasks, such as giving shampoos, or are assigned to perform the simpler hairstyling patterns. Once they have demonstrated their skills, they are gradually permitted to perform the more complicated tasks, such as giving shaves, coloring hair, or applying a permanent.

Personal Trainers

To meet safety and insurance standards and state and local regulations, most health clubs require that instructors and trainers have appropriate qualifications or licenses.

Personal trainers hold a great deal of responsibility for their clients' welfare and must be fully trained in what they do.

There are a few routes trainers can take to learn their craft and become certified. Some universities offer exercise science or exercise physiology programs. You can also do a home study through the American Council on Exercise (ACE), then take the exam they give twice a year. The American College of Sports Medicine (ACSM) is another certifying body. Both tests have written and practical components.

The practical test consists of sub-max testing where you are evaluated while you monitor a client's heart rate and blood pressure. You will also put your client through a work out; your spotting techniques and how you interact will be judged.

A training program can take two to eight weeks, or four years if you pursue a bachelor's degree. And once you have become a personal trainer you'll need continuing education credits to keep up your certification.

JOB OUTLOOK

Overall employment of barbers, cosmetologists, and personal trainers is expected to grow faster than the average for all occupations through the year 2005. Population growth, rising incomes, and a growing demand for the services that they provide will stimulate the demand for these workers. Within this occupation, however, different employment trends are expected.

Cosmetologists will account for virtually all of the employment growth, reflecting the continuing shifts in consumer preferences to more personalized services and in salons to full-service, unisex establishments. Demand for manicurists and for cosmetologists who are trained in nail care will be particularly strong. Employment of barbers is expected to decline slightly.

SALARIES

Barbers and cosmetologists receive income either from commissions and tips or wages and tips. According to limited information, most full-time barbers and cosmetologists earned between $20,000 and $30,000 in 1992, including tips. Earnings depend on the size and location of the shop, the number of hours worked, customers' tipping habits, competition from other barbershops and salons, and the barber's or cosmetologist's ability to attract and keep regular customers.

Personal trainers in a health club can work on commission or an hourly rate and earn anywhere from $45 to $150 an hour, depending upon the budget of the clientele.

Personal trainers can set their own hours, train four people in a day and be done, if they choose. But if they are self-employed, personal trainers need to attend to taxes and insurance expenses, rather than have tax expenses covered by the health club they work for.

RELATED FIELDS

Other workers whose main activity consists of improving a patron's personal appearance include beauty consultants, makeup and wig specialists, and salon and health club managers. Additional workers are employed in the cosmetology industry in such roles as instructors and beauty supply distributors.

INTERVIEW
Michael Silvestri
Hair Stylist

Michael Silvestri has been in the business for over 30 years, both as a salaried hair stylist and the owner of his own salons.

What the Job's Really Like

"It's great, and it's really interesting work. I love people. If you didn't you couldn't stay in this business. Today, most of my best friends are people I've met in the industry, mostly clients.

"The downside of it for me was that I never had as much difficulty with clients as I did with other hair stylists. As a coworker that was easy, but when I was the boss, the hairdressers were very difficult. They're a different breed with their own mind set. I don't know if it was the 'artistic temperament' or what, but so many different things entered into it. For a long time there was a huge drug abuse problem. You find out that one of your top stylists was a drug user–then what are you going to do about it? If you let people go, you're going to lose business. When your hair stylists moved on to another salon they take their clients with them, and there's nothing you could do about that. As an owner, this is always first on your mind. You have to kowtow to very temperamental people and sometimes unreliable people. They wouldn't show up to work or they'd be late, but you couldn't afford to fire them.

"This is one of the reasons I choose not to be an owner anymore. For most of my career I have been an owner, and though I liked it enough to stay with it that long, I have a lot more freedom as an independent hair stylist. For example, I just took my first vacation in nine years. As an owner, you have to always be there, you have to watch what's going on, and you have to watch the register, otherwise you won't make any money. It's largely a cash business. They can take what they want from you and you wouldn't know.

"The advantages, of course, to being an owner is that you have the opportunity to make a lot more money. If it all clicks, you've got it good. When I had the two salons going and we had 26 employees, we were doing very well. And, of course, there's the satisfaction when you do well, starting a business and watching it grow.

"But it fluctuates. There's not much security. Because the employees come and go, you could go from 26 employees down to 15, but you have the same overhead. The hours are terrible and you need a huge financial outlay to start a business. You'd probably need at least $75,000 now to do it.

"When you're not an owner, you can pick and choose where you're going to work, set your own hours. If you don't want to work six hours, you can work four. It's up to you.

"How much money you make depends on how good you are. It also depends on the type of salon you work in. The upscale ones that charge more money for their services are going to generally pay you more. You'd make any combination of a salary, plus commission, plus tips. Commissions can run from 40 to 70 percent. Base salary could be as low as a couple of hundred a week. Just something to get you started. Tips would fluctuate wildly. A shampoo assistant might earn $40 or $50 a week; a hairdresser could pull in as much as $300 or $400 a week.

"In dealing with clients, you have to spend time with them, learn about them, and help them get over any past bad experiences they've had at the hairdressers. You might decide what you believe will look good on them, but then you have to be able to convince them that it will work. Sometimes it takes more than one appointment to get comfortable with each other. One mistake, however, and you could lose that client forever.

"It's very hard work, very tiring work. Most people don't understand that, but you're on your feet all day. Hairdressers wind up with bad backs, or bad necks, or some kind of foot problem. Carpal tunnel syndrome goes with it, too. And I'm allergic to a lot of the products we use, the mousses and gels. My skin will break out and you can't really wear gloves.

"But I love to work with clients, especially new ones. It's great to take someone and make her over, make her look totally different than when she came in. That's the fun part."

How Michael Silvestri Got Started

"I was influenced by family members. My uncle was a men's barber. At the time, I was on Wall Street working as a stock transfer clerk and wasn't very happy. I didn't like the office atmosphere. My uncle would hear me complain when I came home at night and he suggested I go to school. The first thing I thought was, 'Why would I want to do that?' I had no idea that I had an inclination to do that sort of thing. He kept pushing it and after a while he wore me down and I decided to try it.

"So, when I was 17, within seven months after graduating high school, I enrolled in hairdressing school. The program took about a year and I studied at a private academy. That was 1961.

"After I finished, I apprenticed myself. At that time, the only way a male hairdresser could get a job was to sign yourself into servitude. I got a couple of jobs in the area as a shampooer, but worked for free for about nine months. But I really learned, and I also got a few tips here and there. I also took a month's course at Charles of the Ritz in New York, which at the time was considered a very good hair styling academy.

"Then I was finally hired on as a hairdresser at one of the shops I had apprenticed in. That was the start of my career. I worked in a variety of shops, then in 1965 I opened my first shop, and in 1973 I relocated to the south.

"I went to work for a real top-flight guy I had met in Philadelphia and stayed with him for about two years. One of his employees left him to open his own shop and invited me along. I was his operator/manager for about 10 years.

"In 1984 I opened my own shop with a partner and in 1990 we opened another salon. But I wasn't very happy, so in 1994 I sold both shops and went to work as an employee in another salon. And that's what I'm doing now."

Expert Advice

"I used to always give my new employees a talk before they got started. I'd say, 'Remember that the first time you get a new client, she's probably scared to death. She doesn't know you, she doesn't know your place. You've got a strange instrument in your hand–a pair of scissors that can cause some serious damage. People do some crazy things with hair cuts. So, it's up to you to make her comfortable.' A lot of hairdressers don't bother to do that, but I think it's very important for a new client. You have to spend time consulting with them, taking their lifestyle into consideration, the shape of their face, and what kind of hair they have. Then you can go to work, but not before.

"And if you're going into this business, you have to have an independent streak in you, you can't be afraid. You're going to function as an independent contractor for your whole career, so you have to be able to take care of yourself.

"You also have to decide that you're willing to work hard enough to make this work. If you're lazy, you won't make any money. It will take a while to build up a clientele, as well as your skills and confidence. You have to be prepared for at least one or two lean years."

INTERVIEW

Robin Landry
Esthetician

While a cosmetologist is trained primarily in hair care, estheticians work exclusively with skin care. Robin Landry is a skin care professional.

What the Job's Really Like

"First of all, it's a great feeling to make someone feel good. And also to see the results of your work on something as personal as someone's skin. That's very, very personal and I think it takes a little bit of a push to get someone to admit they need help with that, but once they do, they look up to me as someone who *can* help them. And sometimes I'm simply amazed at the results I get.

"It doesn't look as if I work for myself because I operate out of two different salons, but in actuality I do. I'm paid on commission. The salons give me a workplace–I don't have to pay rent or other overhead expenses–and they provide me with all my products and supplies. For that they take a 35 percent cut. I also get tips and a percentage–an average of 15 percent–on the beauty products I sell to my clients.

"In addition, being on the premises provides me with a captive audience, so to speak. But, of course, once they put the clients into my hands, it's up to me to make sure they keep coming back.

"To do that requires professionalism. A lot of people can give a good facial, but a good bedside manner and my professionalism really make a big difference. And, I keep them coming back with a good product. I believe in what I sell and in what I do. That says a lot to my clients.

"Giving the actual facial is a very relaxing hour and fifteen minutes, for both my clients and myself. Clients do remark on that. They're very envious of my silent, quiet job. But they only see that side of it. They don't see the frustrations.

"I work only four days a week. But one of my days is a 12-hour day, another is 9 hours, and the other two are 8 hours. I give myself three days off because you can get very burnt out in this business. The clients drain you of everything you can possibly give. You have at least 20 questions coming out of each client's mouth; they each have their own stories and beliefs on products and ingredients in products. So you really have to stand strong and be knowledgeable. You're always having to defend your position.

"Not only do you have to keep up with your schedule, which can be very hectic; you also have to sell products, and you have to keep a file on each client. This helps you keep track of which treatments you've done on them, which products you've sold to them. And selling the products is very important. Retail is where you make your money. A facial costs about $50, waxing ranges from $8 to $45, and makeup can cost from $25 to $55–but on top of that, some clients might leave with $150 worth of products. You have to have the product in stock, or else you'll lose the sale. The salon shelves should be stocked with these products, but you end up hearing all these sob stories from the owners–when they can order, how much they can afford to order. I do the actual ordering, taking on that responsibility to make sure the orders get into the representatives, but first I have to clear it through the owner.

"Another frustration is with appointments. People don't show up. I've tried to incorporate a policy that they will be billed 50 percent if they don't give me 24-hours notice. I've probably had only one person pay, though. In the end, I don't really enforce it.

"Another difficult aspect is that your performance and your appearance always have to be a "10." That can be tricky keeping yourself together when you're running like a crazy person all day. Your hair falls out of its scrunchy and your lipstick wears off and it's four hours before you have time to put more on. I always make sure to do that, though. I wear a cake powder so my skin always looks good and I make sure I always have lipstick on.

"But it feels good, being your own boss, and being in charge of your own success."

How Robin Landry Got Started

"I was going to school for massage therapy to begin with, but a month or two into the program I fell and broke my wrist. I was out of work and in occupational therapy for two years with that wrist. Finally, I was able to work and I had jobs with a chiropractor and a dentist. I was really involved with one-on-one patient care a lot, and I always liked that. But I did not appreciate not being appreciated. By my employers, that is, not by the patients. So I had to decide to do something for myself, with myself, by myself, and be able to thank myself for it. I decided to go back to school, this time for skin care. And that was only because there was some massage involved in it and I was more impressed with that than any of the other areas of the aesthetic industry.

"I went to a private career institute and studied formally for six months. My areas are mainly skin care, makeup, and waxing. When I finished the program, I took the test and got my license. Since then I've had ongoing training with continuing education courses and seminars through the product manufacturers."

Expert Advice

"I would highly recommend a career in skin care. I consider it more glamorous and less taxing than working with hair and nails.

"And I think you're better off working on a percentage basis than renting the space yourself. I did that the first year and lost some money. You can make a good living but it's unpredictable. You never know how much you're going to earn. You need to give yourself time to gradually and consistently build up your business.

"Above all else, you have to keep yourself knowledgeable about your work and your products. People will believe in you if you show them that you're confident in what you're doing."

INTERVIEW

Frank Cassisa
Certified Personal Trainer

Frank Cassisa is a certified personal trainer at a national health and fitness chain.

What the Job's Really Like

"Fitness instruction is just like computers; it's always changing, there's always something new coming out. To be the best trainer you have to stay on top of everything.

"One of the best settings is working in a health club. You don't have to generate business because the business is already there in the club. You can also have a private practice, at your own place or going to people's homes. But once you're outside of a club setting you're talking totally different insurance coverage. If you work out of your own home or in a client's home you need to cover yourself. You're more open for a lawsuit if something should happen to the client. At a club you come under their insurance.

"I work for a club and I'm covered by their insurance, but even then it doesn't mean someone couldn't come after me personally. But it would have to be plain stupidity to do something that could cause a client to get hurt. Safety is the key.

"We have to check the equipment before the client actually uses that equipment. You have to be fully aware of the human body and how it should move and shouldn't move. If there are any complications or special populations you're working with, for example, diabetics, rehab cardiac patients, people with arthritis, or pregnant women, there are different ways to train them.

"When you're a certified personal trainer you not only know about nutrition and kinesiology, which is the study of the movement of the body and how the muscles react to certain exercises, you also learn first aid. All certified personal trainers must be certified in CPR.

"With the general population, people who want to improve their fitness, you first have to take a health history, get their doctor's name and number and ask the right questions about their age, smoking, any history of health risk factors. If we feel this person is not ready for a training program we'll tell them 'no' and have them contact their doctor for a physical.

"The perfect scenario for someone not ready is the 45-year old male who smokes, is overweight, and somebody in his family had diabetes. This person could be a walking time bomb. It would be up for the doctor to do a stress test and see if he's ready. We don't do any diagnosing; we can only suspect. We're not doctors or dietitians; we have to refer them to professionals if we feel we can't answer their questions or their condition needs medical attention.

"If a client is a go-ahead, we assess him or her and try to get in all the elements of physical fitness, such as flexibility, muscular strength and endurance, cardiovascular endurance, and body composition. Normally a training session is an hour. Clients come once or twice a week to meet with the trainer. And they should come on their own the other days."

How Frank Cassisa Got Started

"For me it's always been my hobby, but now I'm getting paid for it. I studied through ACE and took their two-part exam, a written and a practical. I love to work out and I love to teach people. I work five days a week. When I take my two-hour lunch break I'm working out. You have to be driven and absorb the whole lifestyle."

Expert Advice

"You need a great attitude and you have to practice what you preach. To a client you're a friend, father figure, role model. They'll follow someone who has the results they're looking for.

"Caring is also important. You need a firm hand but diplomatic skills. You're an instructor, not a dictator."

•   •   •

FOR MORE INFORMATION

Lists of barber schools, by state, are available from:

National Association of Barber Schools, Inc.
304 South 11th Street
Lincoln, NE 68502

A list of licensed training schools and licensing requirements for cosmetologists can be obtained from:

National Accrediting Commission of Cosmetology
  Arts and Sciences
901 North Stuart Street, Suite 900
Arlington, VA 22203

Association of Accredited Cosmetology Schools, Inc.
5201 Leesburg Pike
Falls Church, VA 22041

Further information about barber and cosmetology schools also is available from:

Accrediting Commission of Career Schools/
    Colleges of Technology
750 1st Street, N.E., Suite 905
Washington, DC 20002

For details on state licensing requirements and approved barber or cosmetology schools, contact the state board of barber examiners or the state board of cosmetology in your state capital.

For information on training and certification for a career as a personal trainer, contact the following associations:

American Council on Exercise (ACE)
P.O. Box 910449
San Diego, CA 92191
(Provides certification for personal trainers)

American College of Sports Medicine (ACSM)
Member and Chapter Services Department
P.O. Box 1440
Indianapolis, IN 46206

Orthopedic Certification Board (ONCB)
P.O. Box 56
East Holly Avenue
Pitman, NJ 08071

International Physical Fitness Association
415 W. Court Street
Flint, MI 48503

CHAPTER 6 Hotel Personnel

OVERVIEW

The hotel industry is one of the largest employers in the United States. To provide an effective service to vacationers, business travelers, and local and distant enterprises needing meeting and convention space, hotels utilize the services of a variety of managers and assistants.

Hotel managers are responsible for the efficient and profitable operation of their establishments. In a small hotel, motel, or inn with a limited staff, a single manager may direct all aspects of operations. However, large hotels may employ hundreds of workers, and the manager may be aided by a number of assistant managers assigned among departments responsible for various aspects of operations. Assistant managers must see to it that the day-to-day operations of their departments meet the general manager's standards.

EDUCATION
On-the-Job Training Possible
B.A./B.S. Recommended

$$$ SALARY/EARNINGS
$30,000 to $50,000

General Managers

The general manager has overall responsibility for the operation of the hotel. Within guidelines established by the owners of the hotel or executives of the hotel chain, the general manager sets room rates, allocates funds to departments, approves expenditures, and establishes standards for service to guests, decor, housekeeping, food quality, and banquet operations.

Resident Managers

Resident managers live in hotels and are on call 24 hours a day to resolve any problems or emergencies, although they normally work an eight-hour day. As the most senior assistant manager, a resident manager oversees the day-to-day operations of the hotel. In many hotels, the general manager also serves as the resident manager.

Housekeeping

Executive housekeepers are responsible for insuring that guest rooms, meeting and banquet rooms, and public areas are clean, orderly, and well maintained. They train, schedule, and supervise the work of housekeepers; inspect rooms; and order cleaning supplies.

Front Office

Front office managers coordinate reservations and room assignments, and train and direct the hotel's front desk staff that deals with the public. They insure that guests are handled courteously and efficiently, that complaints and problems are resolved, and that requests for special services are carried out.

EDUCATION
B.A./B.S. Recommended
On-the-Job Training Possible

$$$ SALARY/EARNINGS
$30,000 to $50,000

Food and Beverage Managers

Food and beverage managers direct the food services of hotels. They oversee the operation of hotels' restaurants, cocktail lounges, and banquet facilities. They supervise and schedule food and beverage preparation and service workers, plan menus, estimate costs, and deal with food suppliers.

EDUCATION
B.A./B.S. Recommended
On-the-Job Training Possible

$$$ SALARY/EARNINGS
$30,000 to $50,000

Convention Managers

Convention services managers coordinate the activities of large hotels' various departments for meetings, conventions, and other special events. They meet with representatives of groups or organizations to plan the number of rooms to reserve, the desired configuration of hotel meeting space, and any banquet services needed. During the meeting or event, the managers resolve unexpected problems and monitor activities to check that hotel operations conform to the expectations of the group.

Additional Assistant Managers

Other assistant managers may be specialists responsible for activities, such as personnel, accounting and office administration, marketing and sales, purchasing, security, maintenance, and recreational facilities.

TRAINING

In many hotels, on-the-job training is possible at all levels of employment, but completing a formal training program will make you more competitive. Without experience, you might very well get hired, but start at the bottom of the ladder. With a college degree in hotel management or a related field, you could walk into an assistant manager position or be offered a place in a management training program.

Postsecondary training in hotel or restaurant management is preferred for most hotel management positions, although a college liberal arts degree may be sufficient when coupled with related hotel experience. In the past, most managers were promoted from the ranks of front desk clerks, housekeepers, waiters, chefs, and hotel sales workers. Although some people still advance to hotel management positions without the benefit of education or training beyond high school, postsecondary education is increasingly important.

Nevertheless, experience working in a hotel even part-time while in school is an asset to anyone seeking to enter hotel management careers. Restaurant management training or experience is also a good background for entering hotel management, because the success of a hotel's food service and beverage operations is often extremely important to the profitability of the entire establishment.

A bachelor's degree in hotel and restaurant administration provides particularly strong preparation for a career in hotel management. In 1993 over 160 colleges and universities offered bachelor's and graduate programs in this field. Over 800 community and junior colleges, technical institutes, vocational and trade schools, and other academic institutions also have programs leading to an associate degree or other formal recognition in hotel or restaurant management. Graduates of hotel or restaurant management programs usually start as trainee assistant managers, or at least advance to such positions more quickly.

Hotel management programs usually include instruction in hotel administration, accounting, economics, marketing, housekeeping, food service management and catering, hotel maintenance engineering, and data processing (reflecting the widespread use of computers in hotel operations such as reservations). You may also learn accounting, and housekeeping management. Programs encourage interested workers part-time or summer work in hotels and restaurants, because the experience gained and the contacts made with employers may benefit students when they seek full-time employment after graduation.

JOB OUTLOOK

Employment of salaried hotel managers is expected to grow about as fast as the average for all occupations through the year 2005 as more hotels and motels are built. Business travel will continue to grow, and increased domestic and foreign tourism will create additional demand for hotels and motels.

However, manager jobs are expected to grow more slowly than the hotel industry because a growing share of the industry will be comprised of economy properties, which generally have fewer managers than full-service hotels. In the face of financial constraints, guests are becoming more bargain-conscious, and hotel chains are increasing the number of rooms in economy class hotels. Because there are not as many departments in such hotel, fewer managers are needed on the hotel premises.

SALARIES

Salaries of hotel managers vary greatly according to their responsibilities and the size of the hotel in which they work. In 1993 annual salaries of assistant hotel managers averaged an estimated $32,500, according to a survey conducted for the American Hotel and Motel Association. Assistants employed in large hotels with over 350 rooms averaged nearly $38,400 in 1993; those in small hotels with no more than 150 rooms averaged more than $26,000.

Salaries of assistant managers also varied due to differences in duties and responsibilities. For example, food and beverage managers averaged an estimated more than $41,200, whereas front office managers averaged nearly $26,500. The manager's level of experience is another important factor influencing potential income.

In 1993 salaries of general managers averaged more than $59,100–ranging from an average of about $44,900 in hotels and motels with no more than 150 rooms to an average of about $86,700 in large hotels with over 350 rooms. Managers may earn bonuses of up to 15 percent of their basic salary in some hotels. In addition, they and their families may be furnished with lodging, meals, parking, laundry, and other services.

Most managers and assistants receive three to eleven paid holidays a year, as well as paid vacation, sick leave, life insurance, medical benefits, and pension plans. Some hotels offer profit-sharing plans, educational assistance, and other benefits to their employees.

RELATED FIELDS

Hotel managers and assistants are not the only workers concerned with organizing and directing a business in which pleasing people is very important. Others with similar responsibilities include restaurant managers, apartment building managers, retail store managers, and office managers.

INTERVIEW

LeAnne Coury
Assistant Director of Sales

LeAnne Coury has been in the hotel and sales business for 20 years. She works at the Quality Suites Hotel, a national chain, and is responsible for 207 suites and three meeting rooms.

What the Job's Really Like

"Every day is different, not like in some jobs where the work can get monotonous. The hotel industry isn't like that. You might come in in the morning with a plan to work on something specific, then something else comes up and you end up doing that. The meeting planners for a large group convention might come in and want to discuss details with you, so you put your other work on hold for a while.

"Basically, the way it works in the sales end of things is that you're out looking for new business and staying on top of your current business. We look for corporate customers and we want to stay in touch on a regular basis.

"I'm on the phone a lot, checking details, taking care of rooming lists. There are always a lot of details and you have to follow through on promises you make. For example, if you promised to hold 10 two-bedded suites for them, you have to make sure that's what got booked, not 10 king suites. And with conferences, you need to follow up on audiovisual equipment or registration tables, or whatever a particular conference needs.

"I'm up and down a lot, too, not just always sitting at a desk. I walk around the hotel, double check on my groups, make sure they're happy.

"As I said, every day is new because you're working with different people all the time. That's what I think makes it fun.

"But, as with any job, there are always some downsides. Sometimes you get bogged down with paperwork, but if you're an organized person you should be able to stay on top of it. It's not too bad.

"Another aspect of this business is that a hotel never closes, so your hours won't always be the best sometimes. You could be working nights, weekends. However, I think once you put enough time in, you can move into some of the positions where you don't have such a messed up schedule. With a smaller hotel, it's a little easier.

"Still, the advantages far outweigh the disadvantages. In sales you're working with some high-energy people in an up kind of atmosphere. We have bells on our desk and when we book something we ring our bells. Doing sales blitzes is lots of fun, too. We do ours with a theme. The most recent one was called 'We're Fishin' for Your Business.' We had special shirts with fish printed on them, as well as our logo. We also put together what we call a 'blitz bag.' They're plastic bags that we stuff with all sorts of promotional items, such as coasters, rulers, calculators. Then, unannounced, we go out and visit big office buildings. We just walk in and tell them we'd like to be able to work with them, that we're 'fishin' for their business.' We recently hit about three or four hundred businesses in this area. It's a good way to get leads and get your name out there.

"We laugh and have a good time at our job. It's fun to go to work. I've never gotten up in the morning and dreaded going in."

How LeAnne Coury Got Started

"Right out of high school I worked for a chamber of commerce in the convention and sales department. That's where I first got into the convention end. I got to see how they booked the whole city, how they go after major conventions. I worked with booking blocks of hotel rooms city-wide versus working in one specific hotel.

"After about a year there, I realized I wouldn't have a chance for advancement. Hotels offer better opportunities and more money. The experience I got with the chamber of commerce translated well into hotel work.

"I took a position as a sales and catering secretary at the Red Lion Hotel in Oregon. They had about 75 very upscale hotels. I was there only six months and learned everything I could. Then I applied for a position in another hotel that I saw was under construction about two hours away. I sat with the general manager in the coffee shop for an hour or so. He ended up calling me and offering me the sales and convention manager position. It was on a trial basis because of my age; I was only twenty at the time. The drinking age was twenty-one, so they had legal issues to deal with about my selling liquor. That was a great job. They could seat 1,000 and I pretty much ran all of that. I stayed there for three and a half years, but then an opportunity came up for me to go back to Red Lion as the sales and catering manager. It turned out to be a good move for me, with more money, more responsibility. After three years I moved to Alabama, but there weren't as many hotel opportunities there for me, so I went into the legal field for a while and worked as a legal secretary.

"But I missed the hotels. It's usually something you either love or hate, there's no in between. I finally found a job in Mobile, Alabama, and traveled between five different states, promoting the hotel.

"In 1990 I started at the Quality Suites Hotel in Deerfield Beach, Florida. My first position was as sales and catering manager. Later I moved up to my current position, assistant director of sales. The next step up for me would be as director of sales, then I could even think about moving into a general manager position. The opportunities are there and they're willing to train you."

Expert Advice

"If you're going into this industry you have to like people and have a happy personality. You have to be able to always have a smile on your face, and if a guest or a customer is dissatisfied you have to be able to handle it. You don't ever want to lose business.

"You have to be a team player, too. If the restaurant gets busy, for example, I'll go over and help them out there. If someone needs help, then that's what you do. Our job descriptions aren't rigidly set. But it's fun to do something different once in a while.

"Another thing, when you're looking for work, you'll probably be better off working for a hotel that is corporate owned rather than a family-owned franchise. There'll be more opportunities for you to move up and probably better salaries.

"But don't get discouraged when you're starting out at the bottom. For example, a position at the front desk might not be the highest paying job, but it's a good way to learn."

INTERVIEW

Missy Soleau
Food and Beverage Manager

In just five years, Missy Soleau worked her way up the ladder from busing tables to a position as food and beverage manager at the Quality Suites Hotel. She and LeAnne Coury (profiled in the previous interview) work at the same property.

What the Job's Really Like

"I do a hundred different things and wear a lot of different hats. I'm responsible for all the scheduling of the kitchen staff, and all the ordering and purchasing of the food and other supplies. Because it's such a small property, I'm also responsible for the banquet end of things. I do the bookings, the set-ups, and the clean-ups.

"No day is ever the same. I could be serving coffee in the morning, then participate in an executive meeting in the afternoon. And it could be that I'm here from 5:30 in the morning to 11 o'clock at night. I like to get here early in the morning, so if I do have a banquet or another event scheduled I can see that everything is going as planned. The meeting might run until 5 P.M., then I have to clean up and then get the room ready for another meeting that might start at 6 P.M. I do have a little bit of help here, but most of the time I do it by myself. Because of the small staff we have, there's a lot of moving and lifting. The tables are heavy. I work six days a week, anywhere from 50 to 60 hours a week. I enjoy it, maybe because it keeps me out of trouble.

"I'm paid on a salary basis, no overtime, but if I take a day off I'm not docked. I started as an assistant food and beverage manager at an hourly wage of about $6.50. I was determined, though. Now, it all adds up to about $22,800 a year, plus gratuities from the banquets.

"It's below what it should be, but the experience is what I'm looking for. All my training is on the job. This company is growing—we just purchased our fiftieth hotel (although there are hundreds, maybe thousands of franchised Quality Suites across the country)—so I can stay with them and move to a bigger hotel. I'm flexible and able to move anywhere. If I did go to a larger hotel, I'd probably start back as assistant manager again, but the salary would probably be more than I'm earning now.

"It's very challenging work with lots of variation. I've been here three years and the same people come back and I really enjoy seeing them every year and catching up with them."

How Missy Soleau Got Started

"I had been in the retail business since I was 16, but decided I'd like to try the hotel and restaurant field. I started four or five years ago busing tables. I just walked into a hotel's restaurant and applied for a job. About a month later I became a waitress.

"After Hurricane Andrew I lost my job because the hotel had structural damage. I heard that the Quality Suites was hiring and

I started here as a hostess in August, 1992. I worked closely with the food and beverage manager; he needed some help because the hurricane had filled up the hotel. Then I was promoted to assistant food and beverage manager, and in December of 1994, when he left, I moved into his position.

"After high school I went to a small trade school and received my associate's degree in business administration/travel and tourism in 1990. My original plan was to work in the travel industry. But rather than sitting behind a desk taking reservations, I realized I'd prefer working directly with the people. I'm more of a people person than a phone person, definitely right for the restaurant business. It just so happened that I got a job at a hotel restaurant and it's worked out really well. I know now I prefer working in a hotel rather than in just a restaurant.

"People here are on vacation and they really want to be catered to. Their needs are different from people who live in the area and are just going out to dinner. A lot of them are here for long periods of time, especially during the season, so you get to know them on a more personal basis. Working in a restaurant, you'd just see them that one night."

Expert Advice

"I have no formal training in food and beverage, but I would recommend that anyone wanting to go into this field should go to school and get a degree. Hands-on training is best, I think, but in the long run, formal training can really make a difference.

"Another thing I think I would like to do is go to chef school. Even if you don't plan to work full-time as a chef, it's a good skill to have. As food and beverage manager, you might have to step in and take over if your chef is out unexpectedly. And also, if you understand what's involved for a cook, you can share ideas and work better together.

"And be prepared to start off at a low salary. Eventually you'll be able to work your way up."

● ● ●

FOR MORE INFORMATION

For information on careers and scholarships in hotel management, contact:

The American Hotel and Motel Association (AH&MA)
Information Center
1201 New York Avenue, N.W.
Washington, DC 20005-3931

For information on educational programs, including correspondence courses, in hotel and restaurant management, write to:

The Educational Institute of AH&MA
P.O. Box 1240
East Lansing, MI 48826

For information on careers in housekeeping management, contact:

National Executive Housekeepers Association, Inc.
1001 Eastwind Drive, Suite 301
Westerville, OH 43081

For information on hospitality careers, as well as how to purchase a directory of colleges and other schools offering programs and courses in hotel and restaurant administration, write to:

Council on Hotel, Restaurant, and Institutional Education
1200 17th Street, N.W.
Washington, DC 20036-3097

CHAPTER 7 Restaurant Personnel

OVERVIEW

Eating establishments range from restaurants that serve fast food or those that emphasize elegant dining to institutional dining in school and employee cafeterias, hospitals, and nursing facilities. The cuisine offered, its price, and the setting in which it is consumed may vary greatly, but the employees of these diverse dining facilities have many responsibilities in common.

Efficient and profitable operation of restaurants and institutional food service facilities requires managers and assistant managers to select and appropriately price interesting menu items, efficiently use food and other supplies, achieve consistent quality in food preparation and service, recruit and train adequate numbers of workers and supervise their work, and attend to the various administrative aspects of the business.

Restaurant Managers

In most restaurants the manager is assisted by one or more assistant managers, depending on the size and business hours of the establishment. In large establishments, as well as in many others that offer fine dining, the management team consists of a general manager, one or more assistant managers, and an executive chef.

In fast-food restaurants and other food service facilities that operate long hours, seven days a week, the manager is aided by several assistant managers, each of whom supervises a shift of workers.

EDUCATION
On-the-Job Training Possible
A.A./A.S. Recommended
B.A./B.S. Recommended

$$$ SALARY/EARNINGS
$25,000 to $45,000

Managers interview, hire, and, when necessary, discharge workers. They familiarize newly hired workers with the establishment's policies and practices, and oversee their training. Managers schedule the work hours of employees, ensuring that there are enough workers present during busy periods, but not too many during slow periods.

Restaurant and food service managers supervise the kitchen and the dining room. They oversee food preparation and cooking, checking the quality of the food and the sizes of portions to insure that dishes are prepared and garnished correctly and get to the table in a timely manner. They also investigate and resolve customers' complaints about food quality or service. During busy periods, managers may roll up their sleeves and help with the cooking, clearing of tables, or other tasks. They direct the cleaning of the kitchen and dining areas and the washing of tableware, kitchen utensils, and equipment to maintain company and government sanitation standards. They monitor workers and observe patrons on a continual basis to ensure compliance with health and safety standards and local liquor regulations.

Managers have a variety of administrative responsibilities. In larger establishments, much of this work is delegated to a bookkeeper; in others, managers must keep accurate records of the hours and wages of employees, prepare the payroll, and do paperwork to comply with licensing laws and reporting requirements of tax, wage and hour, unemployment compensation, and Social Security laws. They also must maintain records of the costs of supplies and equipment purchased and ensure that accounts with suppliers are paid on a regular basis. Moreover, managers record the number, type, and cost of items; and weed out dishes that are unpopular or less profitable. Many managers are able to ease the burden of recordkeeping and paperwork through the use of computers.

Managers are among the first to arrive and the last to leave at night. At the conclusion of each day (or each shift), managers must tally the cash received and charge receipts and balance them against the record of sales. They are responsible for depositing the day's income at the bank or securing it in a safe place. Managers are also responsible for locking up; checking that ovens, grills, and lights are off; and switching on alarm systems.

Ordering supplies and dealing with suppliers are important aspects of restaurant and food service managers.

Executive Chefs

The executive chef oversees the operation of the kitchen, while the assistant managers oversee service in the dining room and other areas of the operation. In some smaller restaurants, the executive chef may also be the general manager, and sometimes is an owner.

🎓 EDUCATION

On-the-Job Training Possible
A.A./A.S. Recommended
B.A./B.S. Recommended

$$$ SALARY/EARNINGS

$30,000 to $40,00 for
experienced chefs
$5.00 to $7.00 per hour for
other kitchen workers

Chefs and Cooks

A reputation for serving good food is essential to any restaurant, whether it prides itself on hamburgers and French fries or exotic foreign cuisine. Chefs, cooks, and other kitchen workers are largely responsible for a restaurant's reputation. Some restaurants offer a varied menu featuring meals that are time-consuming and difficult to prepare, and that require a highly skilled cook or chef. Other restaurants emphasize fast service, offering hamburgers and sandwiches that can be prepared in advance or in a few minutes by a fast-food or short-order cook with only limited cooking skills.

Chefs and cooks are responsible for preparing meals that are tasty and attractively presented. Chefs are the most highly skilled, trained, and experienced kitchen workers. Although the terms "chef" and "cook" are still sometimes used interchangeably, cooks generally have more limited skills. Many chefs have earned fame for both themselves and the restaurants, hotels, and institutions where they work because of their skill in artfully preparing the traditional favorites and in creating new dishes and improving familiar ones.

Menu Planners

While many restaurants rarely change their menu, other eating establishments change theirs frequently. Institutional food service facilities and some restaurants offer a new menu every day. Managers, menu planners, or executive chefs select menu items, taking into account the likely number of customers, the past popularity of various dishes, and other considerations, such as food left over from prior meals that should not be wasted, the need for variety on the menu, and the availability of foods due to seasonal and other factors. Menu planners analyze the recipes of the dishes to determine food, labor, and overhead costs and assign prices to the menu items. Menus must be developed far enough in advance for needed supplies to be ordered and received in time.

Kitchen Workers

Under the direction of chefs and cooks, other kitchen workers perform tasks requiring less skill. They weigh and measure ingredients, fetch pots and pans, and stir and strain soups and sauces. They clean, peel, and slice vegetables and fruits and make salads. They also may cut and grind meats, poultry, and seafood in preparation for cooking. Their responsibilities also include cleaning work areas, equipment and utensils, and dishes and silverware.

The number and types of workers employed in kitchens depend partly on the type of restaurant. For example, fast-food outlets offer only a few items, which are prepared by fast-food cooks. Smaller, full-service restaurants that offer casual dining often feature a limited number of easy-to-prepare items, supplemented by short-order specialties and readymade desserts. Typically, one cook prepares all of the food with the help of a short-order cook and one or two other kitchen workers.

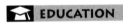
EDUCATION
On-the-Job Training Possible

$$$ SALARY/EARNINGS
$200 to $300 per week

Waiters and Waitresses

Working conditions for waiters and waitresses can vary considerably, depending on where they work. In coffee shops, they are expected to provide fast and efficient, yet courteous, service. In fine restaurants, where gourmet meals are accompanied by attentive formal service, waiters and waitresses serve the meal at a more leisurely pace and offer more personal service to patrons. For example, they may recommend a certain kind of wine as a complement to a particular entree, explain how various items on the menu are prepared, or prepare some salads and other special dishes at tableside.

Depending on the type of restaurant, waiters and waitresses may perform duties associated with other food and beverage service occupations, in addition to waiting on tables. These tasks may include escorting guests to tables, serving customers seated at counters, setting up and clearing tables, or cashiering. However, larger or more formal restaurants frequently relieve their waiters and waitresses of these additional duties.

Bartenders

Bartenders fill the drink orders that waiters and waitresses take from customers seated in the restaurant or lounge, as well as fill orders from customers seated at the bar. Because some people like their cocktails made a certain way, bartenders occasionally are asked to mix drinks to suit a customer's taste. Most bartenders must know dozens of drink recipes and be able to mix drinks accurately, quickly, and without waste, even during the busiest periods.

Besides mixing and serving drinks, bartenders collect payment, operate the cash register, clean up after customers have left, and may also serve food items to customers seated at the bar.

Bartenders who work at service bars have little contact with customers. They work at small bars in restaurants, hotels, and clubs where drinks are served only to diners at tables. However, the majority of bartenders work in eating and drinking establishments where, they also directly serve and socialize with patrons.

Some establishments, especially larger ones, use automatic equipment to mix drinks of varying complexity at the push of a button. However, bartenders still must be efficient and know how to prepare drinks not handled by the automatic equipment, or mix drinks when it is not functioning. Also, equipment is no substitute for the friendly socializing most customers prefer.

Bartenders usually are responsible for ordering and maintaining an inventory of liquor, mixes, and other bar supplies. They also arrange the bottles and glassware into attractive displays and often wash glassware used at the bar.

Hosts and Hostesses

Hosts and hostesses try to evoke a good impression of the restaurant by warmly welcoming guests. They courteously direct patrons to where they can leave their coats and other personal items, and indicate where patrons may wait until their table is ready. Hosts and hostesses assign guests to tables suitable for the size of their group, escort them to their seats, and provide menus.

Hosts and hostesses are restaurants' personal representatives to patrons. They try to ensure that service is prompt and courteous and the meal enjoyable; they may also adjust complaints of dissatisfied diners. Hosts and hostesses schedule dining reservations, arrange parties, and organize any special services that are required. In some restaurants, they also act as cashier.

TRAINING

Restaurant and Food Service Management

Many restaurant and food service manager positions are filled by promoting experienced food and beverage preparation and service workers. Waiters, waitresses, chefs, and fast-food workers who have demonstrated their potential for handling increased responsibility sometimes advance to assistant manager or management trainee jobs when openings occur.

Executive chefs need extensive experience working as a chef; general managers need experience working as an assistant manager.

Most food service management companies and national or regional restaurant chains also recruit management trainees from among the graduates of two-year and four-year college programs. Food service and restaurant chains prefer to hire persons with degrees in restaurant and institutional food service management, but they often hire graduates with degrees in other fields who have a demonstrated interest and aptitude in food service management.

A bachelor's degree in restaurant and food service management provides a particularly strong preparation for a career in this occupation. In 1992, more than 160 colleges and universities offered four-year programs in restaurant and hotel management or institutional food service management. For persons who do not want to pursue a four-year degree, a good alternative is provided by the more than 800 community and junior colleges, technical institutes, and other institutions that offer programs in these fields leading to an associate degree or other formal award below the bachelor's degree.

Both two-year and four-year programs provide instruction in subjects such as accounting, business law and management, food planning and preparation, and nutrition. Some programs combine classroom and laboratory study with internships that provide on-the-job experience. In addition, many educational institutions offer culinary programs that provide food preparation training, which can lead to a career as a cook or chef and provide a foundation for advancement to an executive chef position.

Most restaurant chains and food service management companies have rigorous training programs for persons hired for management jobs. Through a combination of classroom and on-the-job training, trainees receive instruction and gain work experience in all aspects of the operations of a restaurant or institutional food service facility: food preparation, nutrition, sanitation, security, company policies and procedures, personnel management, recordkeeping, and preparation of reports. Usually after six months or a year, trainees receive their first permanent assignment as an assistant manager.

A measure of professional achievement for restaurant and food service managers is to earn the designation of certified Foodservice Management Professional (FMP). Although not a requirement for employment or advancement in the occupation, voluntary certification provides recognition of professional competence, particularly for managers who acquired their skills largely on the job. The Educational Foundation of the National Restaurant Association awards the FMP designation to managers who achieve a qualifying score on a written examination, complete a series of courses that cover a range of food service management topics, and who meet standards of work experience in the field.

Kitchen Workers

Most kitchen workers start as fast-food or short-order cooks, or in one of the other less skilled kitchen positions that require little education or training and that allow them to acquire their skills on the job. After acquiring some basic food handling, preparation, and cooking skills, they may be able to advance to an assistant cook or short-order cook position, but many years of training and experience are necessary to achieve the level of skill required of an executive chef or cook in a fine restaurant.

Even though a high school diploma is not required for beginning jobs, it is recommended for those planning a career as a cook or chef. High school or vocational school courses in business arithmetic and business administration are particularly helpful.

Chefs and Cooks

An increasing number of chefs and cooks are obtaining their training through high school or post-high school vocational programs and two- or four-year colleges. Chefs and cooks may also be trained in apprenticeship programs offered by professional culinary institutes, industry associations, and trade unions. One such program is the three-year apprenticeship program administered by local chapters of the American Culinary Federation, in cooperation with local employers and junior colleges or vocational education institutions. In addition, some large hotels and restaurants operate their own training programs for cooks and chefs.

People who have had courses in commercial food preparation may be able to start in a cook or chef job without having to spend time in a lower skilled kitchen job; they may have an advantage when looking for jobs in better restaurants and hotels, where hiring standards often are high. Some vocational programs in high schools offer this kind of training, but usually these courses are given by trade schools, vocational centers, colleges, professional associations, and trade unions. Postsecondary courses range from a few months to two years or more and in some cases are open only to high school graduates. The armed forces also are a good source of training and experience.

Although curricula may vary, students usually spend most of their time learning to prepare food through actual practice. They learn to bake, broil, and otherwise prepare food, and to use and care for kitchen equipment. Training programs often include courses in menu planning, determination of portion size and food cost control, purchasing food supplies in quantity, selection and storage of food, and use of leftover food to minimize waste. Students also learn hotel and restaurant sanitation and public health rules for handling food. Training in supervisory and management skills is sometimes emphasized in courses offered by private vocational schools, professional associations, and university programs.

Culinary courses are given by 550 schools across the nation. The American Culinary Federation accredited 70 of these programs in 1993. Accreditation is an indication that a culinary program meets recognized standards regarding course content, facilities, and quality of instruction. The American Culinary Federation has only been accrediting culinary programs for a relatively short time, however, and many programs have not yet sought accreditation.

Certification provides valuable formal recognition of the skills of a chef or cook. The American Culinary Federation certifies chefs and cooks at the levels of *cook, working chef, executive chef,* and *master chef.* It also certifies *pastry professionals* and *culinary educators.* Certification standards are based primarily on experience and formal training.

Advancement opportunities for chefs and cooks are better than for most other food and beverage preparation and service occupations. Many acquire higher paying positions and new cooking skills by moving from one job to another. Besides culinary skills, advancement also depends on ability to supervise other workers and limit food costs by minimizing waste and accurately anticipating the amount of perishable supplies needed.

Some cooks and chefs gradually advance to executive chef positions or supervisory or management positions, particularly in hotels, clubs, or larger, more elegant restaurants. Some eventually go into business as caterers or restaurant owners; others may become instructors in vocational programs in high schools, junior and community colleges, and other academic institutions.

Food and Beverage Servers

There are no specific educational requirements for food and beverage service jobs. Although many employers prefer to hire high school graduates for waiter and waitress, bartender, and host and hostess positions, completion of high school is generally not required for fast-food workers, counter attendants, and dining room attendants and bartender helpers. For many persons, a job as a food and beverage service worker serves as a source of immediate income rather than a career. Many entrants to these jobs are in their late teens or early twenties and have a high school education or less. Usually, they have little or no work experience. Many are full-time students or homemakers. Food and beverage service jobs are a major source of part-time employment for high school students.

Most employers place an emphasis on personal qualities. Food and beverage service workers should be well-spoken and have a neat and clean appearance, because they are in close and constant contact with the public. They should enjoy dealing with all kinds of people, and need to have a pleasant disposition and sense of humor. State laws often require that food and beverage service workers obtain health certificates showing that they are free of contagious diseases.

Generally, bartenders must be at least 21 years of age, and many employers prefer to hire persons who are 25 or older. Bartenders should be familiar with state and local laws concerning the sale of alcoholic beverages.

Most food and beverage service workers pick up their skills on the job by observing and working with more experienced workers. Some employers, particularly at fast-food restaurants, use self-instruction programs to teach new employees food preparation and service skills through audiovisual presentations and instructional booklets. Some public and private vocational schools, restaurant associations, and large restaurant chains also provide classroom training in a generalized food service curriculum.

Many bartenders acquire their skills by attending a bartending school or taking vocational and technical school courses that include instruction on state and local laws and regulations, cocktail recipes, attire and conduct, and stocking a bar. Some of these schools help their graduates find jobs.

Due to the relatively small size of most food-serving establishments, opportunities for promotion are limited. After gaining some experience, some dining room and cafeteria attendants and bartender helpers are able to advance to waiter, waitress, or bartender jobs.

For waiters, waitresses, and bartenders, advancement usually is limited to finding a job in a larger restaurant or bar where they can earn more in tips. Some bartenders open their own businesses, and some hosts and hostesses and waiters and waitresses advance to supervisory jobs, such as maitre d'hotel, dining room supervisor, or restaurant manager. In larger restaurant chains, food and beverage service workers who excel at their work are often invited to enter the company's formal management training program.

JOB OUTLOOK

Restaurant and Food Service Managers

Employment of restaurant and food service managers is expected to increase much faster than the average for all occupations through the year 2005. In addition to growth in demand for these managers, the need to replace managers who transfer to other occupations or stop working will create many job openings. Job opportunities are expected to be best for persons with bachelor's or associate's degrees in restaurant and institutional food service management.

Employment growth is expected to vary by industry. Eating and drinking places will provide the most new jobs as the number of eating and drinking establishments increases and other industries continue to contract out their food services. Population growth, rising personal incomes, and increased leisure time will continue to produce growth in the number of meals consumed outside the home. To meet the growing demand for prepared food, more restaurants will be built, and more managers will be employed to supervise them.

In addition, as schools, hospitals, and other businesses increasingly contract out more of their food services to institutional food services companies, the number of manager jobs will grow.

Employment of wage and salary managers is expected to increase more rapidly than self-employed managers. New restaurants are increasingly affiliated with national chains rather than being independently owned and operated. As this trend continues, fewer owners will manage restaurants themselves, and more restaurant managers will be employed to run the establishments.

Employment in eating and drinking establishments is not very sensitive to changes in economic conditions, so restaurant and food service managers are rarely laid off during hard times.

However, competition among restaurants is always intense, and many restaurants do not survive.

Chefs, Cooks, Kitchen Workers, and Food and Beverage Servers

Job openings for chefs, cooks, and other kitchen workers are expected to be excellent through the year 2005. Growth in demand for these workers will create many new jobs, but most openings will arise from the need to replace the relatively high proportion of workers who leave this very large occupation each year. There is substantial turnover in many of these jobs because their limited requirements for formal education and training allow easy entry, and the many part-time positions are attractive to persons seeking a short-term source of income rather than a career. Many of the workers who leave these jobs transfer to other occupations, while others stop working to assume household responsibilities or to attend school full time.

Workers under the age of 25 have traditionally filled a significant proportion of the lesser skilled jobs in this occupation. The pool of young workers is expected to continue to shrink through the 1990s, but begin to grow after the year 2000. Many employers will be forced to offer higher wages, better benefits, and more training to attract and retain workers in these jobs.

EARNINGS

Restaurant and Food Service Managers

Median earnings for restaurant and food service managers were $418 a week in 1992. The middle 50 percent earned between about $300 and $600 a week. The lowest paid 10 percent earned $225 a week or less, while the highest paid 10 percent earned over $815 a week.

Earnings of restaurant and food service managers vary greatly, according to their responsibilities and the type and size of establishment. Based on a survey conducted for the National Restaurant Association, the median base salary of managers in restaurants was estimated to be about $27,900 a year in 1993, but managers of the largest restaurants and institutional food service facilities often had annual salaries in excess of $45,000.

Managers of fast-food restaurants had an estimated median base salary of $24,900 a year; managers of full-menu restaurants with table service, almost $30,400; and managers of commercial and institutional cafeterias, nearly $29,300 a year in 1993. Besides a salary, most managers received an annual bonus or incentive payment based on their performance; most of these payments ranged between $2,000 and $8,000 a year.

Executive chefs had an estimated median base salary of about $33,600 a year in 1993, but those employed in the largest restaurants and institutional food service facilities often had base salaries over $49,000. Annual bonus or incentive payments of executive chefs ranged between $2,000 and $4,000 a year.

The estimated median base salary of assistant managers was over $23,400 a year in 1993, but ranged from less than $19,800 in fast-food restaurants to over $31,700 in some of the largest restaurants and food service facilities. Annual bonus or incentive payments of most assistant managers ranged between $1,000 and $4,000 a year.

Manager trainees had an estimated median base salary of about $20,200 a year in 1993, but had salaries of nearly $27,900 in some of the largest restaurants and food service facilities. Annual bonus or incentive payments of most trainees ranged between $1,000 and $3,000 a year.

Most salaried restaurant and food service managers received free meals, sick leave, health and life insurance, and one to three weeks of paid vacation a year, depending on length of service.

Chefs, Cooks, and Other Kitchen Workers

The wages of chefs, cooks, and other kitchen workers vary depending on the part of the country and, especially, the type of establishment in which they work. Wages generally are highest in elegant restaurants and hotels, and many executive chefs earn over $40,000 annually.

According to a survey conducted by the National Restaurant Association, most cooks earned between $6.00 and $8.00 per hour in 1992. Assistant cooks earned between $5.50 and $6.50 per hour.

According to the same survey, short-order cooks earned between $5.00 and $6.75 an hour; bread and pastry bakers earned within the range of $6.00 to $7.00 per hour. Salad preparation workers generally earned less; most earned between $5.00

and $6.00. Most food preparation workers in fast-food restaurants earned between $4.25 and $5.30 per hour.

Some employers provide uniforms and free meals, but federal law permits employers to deduct from wages the cost, or fair value, of any meals or lodging provided, and some employers exercise this right.

Chefs, cooks, and other kitchen workers who work full time often receive paid vacation, sick leave, and health insurance, but part-time workers generally do not receive such benefits.

In some large hotels and restaurants, kitchen workers belong to unions. The principal unions are the Hotel Employees and Restaurant Employees International Union and the Service Employees International Union.

Food and Beverage Servers

Food and beverage service workers derive their earnings from a combination of hourly wages and customer tips. Their wages and the amount of tips they receive vary greatly, depending on the type of job and establishment. For example, fast-food workers and hosts and hostesses generally do not receive tips, so their wage rates may be higher than those of waiters and waitresses, who may earn more from tips than from wages.

In some restaurants, waiters and waitresses contribute a portion of their tips to a tip pool, which is distributed among many of the establishment's other food and beverage service workers and kitchen staff. Tip pools allow workers who normally do not receive tips, such as dining room attendants, to share in the rewards for a meal well served.

In 1992, median weekly earnings (including tips) of full-time waiters and waitresses were about $220. The middle 50 percent earned between $180 and $300; the top 10 percent earned at least $380 a week.

For most waiters and waitresses, higher earnings are primarily the result of receiving more in tips rather than higher hourly wages. Tips generally average between 10 and 20 percent of guests' checks, so waiters and waitresses working in busy, expensive restaurants earn the most.

Full-time bartenders had median weekly earnings (including tips) of about $250 in 1992. The middle 50 percent earned from $200 to $330; the top 10 percent earned at least $440 a week. Like waiters and waitresses, bartenders employed in public bars may receive more than half of their earnings as tips. Service bartenders are often paid higher hourly wages to offset their lower tip earnings.

Median weekly earnings (including tips) of full-time dining room attendants and bartender helpers were about $210 in 1992. The middle 50 percent earned between $175 and $275; the top 10 percent earned over $350 a week. Most received over half of their earnings as wages; the rest of their income came from their share of the proceeds from tip pools.

In some large restaurants and hotels, food and beverage service workers belong to unions. The principal unions are the Hotel Employees and Restaurant Employees International Union and the Service Employees International Union.

RELATED FIELDS

Restaurant Managers direct the activities of business establishments that provide a service to customers. Other managers in service-oriented businesses include hotel managers and assistants, health services administrators, retail store managers, and bank managers.

Cooks and Chefs are not limited to working in restaurants. Other settings where opportunities exist for food preparers are: hospitals, nursing facilities, schools, military bases, private homes, and corporate offices and employee cafeterias.

Food Servers find employment related to restaurant work as flight attendants, butlers, and diet technicians and diet aides working in hospitals.

INTERVIEW

Linda Dickinson
Chef and Menu Planner at Moosewood Restaurant

In 1973 Moosewood Restaurant, in Ithaca, New York, opened its doors as a collectively run vegetarian eating establishment. Part of the counter-culture at the time, Moosewood workers were early adherents to the now popular philosophy that food could be healthful and taste good at the same time. They also felt that the workplace should be a fun place to be, with all business decisions made jointly.

Moosewood is not operated along the lines of traditional restaurants. At present, 18 women and men rotate through the jobs necessary to make a restaurant go: planning menus, preparing and serving food, setting long-term goals—and washing pots. Their ranks are bolstered by about half a dozen employees.

Most of the Moosewood collective have worked together for over 10 years, and several since the restaurant's early days.

Moosewood was at first known only locally. Now, two decades and several highly acclaimed cookbooks later, Moosewood's reputation for serving fine food in a friendly atmosphere has spread nationally.

Linda Dickinson began working at Moosewood in 1973. She started as a waitress, but soon took on the responsibilities of chef and menu planner. She is also coauthor of New Recipes From Moosewood Restaurant, Sundays At Moosewood Restaurant, and Moosewood Restaurant Cooks At Home.

What the Job's Really Like

"When we're not working on a cookbook, I put in 20 to 30 hours a week at the restaurant. When we are writing, I generally never work less than two shifts or 12 to 14 hours. A menu planning week is closer to 30 or 40 hours, depending on how busy we are.

"This situation is really very different than what most people would encounter. Most people with a cooking position in a traditional restaurant would have to put in more hours than that. That was part of the reason Moosewood was formed as a collective. We wanted to be able to have time to do other things, so our scheduling is flexible and it varies from week to week.

"The first thing I do when I go into work is talk to the menu planner, who lets you know what is planned for the meal you're doing. There's always at least one other cook, sometimes two other cooks, depending on what season it is and how busy we're going to be.

"You consult with the other cooks, too, to see who wants to do what, so you can divide up the tasks. Then you start working. We have soups to prepare, salads, and entrees. I might have to make one soup and two entrees–it depends on how many cooks we have that day. You spend the next three hours cooking until you're open for business. Once we're open, I spend the rest of the time serving the food onto plates so the waiters can take it to the customers.

"The days I'm menu planning, I'm not cooking. I plan the menu according to the season, trying to get a balance of different dishes, some dairy with eggs and cheese, some dishes that are suitable for vegans—vegetarians who don't eat any eggs or dairy products. You want to also balance the dishes according to spicy and not spicy, and you think about the weather. If it's really hot, you might offer something like chilled soup and a salad plate.

"You have to check to see what supplies you have on hand, what you're running low on, what you need to order. You do clean up, you put away deliveries when they come, and you take charge of cleaning out the refrigerators.

"I usually put the order in the night before. We have various suppliers who bring different things. A lot of different orders go in during the week for basic supplies, and every day we order from our produce supplier.

"Moosewood is not a normal cooking situation. We have much more freedom. In a big place, you might be doing line cooking, performing one particular task over and over. There'd be a hierarchy to deal with, too.

"We have a much friendlier situation, which doesn't mean it's not a high-pressured job. When you're in the kitchen and it's very busy you don't get break time. You have to stay until the food is ready and the people have been served. Often you're on your feet all day. It's a high intensity situation. You can be under a lot of pressure. You could run out of food in the middle of a shift and have to start making more. If you don't have enough ingredients for the same dish, you might have to change the menu if you run out. You could burn things, then have to start over.

"As in any profession, there can be tensions among coworkers, and then there's the heat in the kitchen to deal with. Even though we have air conditioning it gets very hot with the ovens going. If you're a cook, you have to expect to be hot a lot. We expanded the restaurant and kitchen area recently, but it's still hot and crowded in there. And it's physically demanding work, lifting heavy pots.

"But I'm happy with the niche I've found. Cooking seems more real to me than sitting in an office doing paperwork. You're producing a product, you're doing your best to make it good, and you're serving it to people who you hope will agree with your taste. You're trying to make food that looks appealing and tastes good. It's a real activity—you're taking care of a basic need in life. People need to eat. So there's the satisfaction in producing a product and having it be well received.

"In general, our group of people is pretty congenial, so you can have fun while you're working, talking with the other like-minded people. In this sort of restaurant it's like being with an extended family.

"But sometimes we get irritable customers and that can be annoying. The waiters will come back and report that someone was unhappy. I usually don't take it personally, but still, one always prefers to hear good things. But since we've been in business as long as we have and we're popular, we get much more good feedback than bad."

How Linda Dickinson Got Started

"In 1968 I got my B.A. in German Literature from Harper College, which is now called SUNY Binghamton. But there were no jobs in German literature.

"Originally, I wasn't attracted to the profession—I fell into it. I waitressed at various places, then in 1973 I started at Moosewood as a waitress. The group had already opened the restaurant a couple of months earlier. As new people came in, they included them in the decision-making process.

"After I waitressed for a while at Moosewood, I told them I knew how to make curries. Because it was a very loose kind of restaurant and nobody had gone to cooking school–they were basically home cooks, not professional–when they heard that I could make curries, they had me come into the kitchen. It was obvious I had more of an aptitude for cooking than I did for waitressing. I was attracted to cooking; I liked playing with the different seasonings. For example, with Indian food there are a lot of exotic combinations that interested me. By learning that skill on my own, it got me into the slot at Moosewood.

"In the early days, everybody who knew how to do certain dishes would teach the other cooks those dishes. I would teach other people about making curries and they would teach me their dishes. And we were all reading cookbooks and learning how to do more things on our own.

"Because our menu changes with every meal, someone has to be in charge of planning what we would have and ordering the food for us. After the first year or two it evolved that a group of menu planners was formed and I became one of them."

Expert Advice

"Some places won't hire you unless you have formal training, while other places will. First, try to figure out what sort of cook or chef you want to be. For some jobs, formal training is a necessity.

"The more experience you can get on your own, cooking at home, cooking for your friends, or observing a cook in your family–the more you can learn about cooking in general–the better it will be. But the fancier expensive places are going to want formal training.

"If there's a restaurant you like to go to, you could talk to some of the people who work there or the owners to see what the requirements are.

"I'm sure there are other places, like Moosewood, that hire people not because they have some sort of formal training, but because they have a feeling for food. We would consider that more important. Sometimes we have had people who've gone to culinary school and they don't work out in our kind of setting. Some of these schools are very rigid in what they teach. Things have to be done in a certain way. We don't necessarily agree with that.

"You can also take a cooking class through adult education or at a community college or with an individual who would offer a course in a particular type of cooking.

"I think cooking can be a very rewarding profession. Although Moosewood isn't high paying, some other restaurants can be. And it can lead to other things, too. You could open your own restaurant or put together a cookbook. There are a lot of restaurants in the world so there are a lot of opportunities."

INTERVIEW
Laura Craycraft
Waitress

Laura Craycraft has been a waitress at the Roadhouse Grill, a new chain in the southeast, since January, 1995. The restaurant has a friendly, "down home" atmosphere, with peanut shells on the floor and lots of interesting western memorabilia.

What the Job's Really Like

"It has it's moments. You can't please all of the people all the time, just some of the people some of the time. You try to deal with it as best as you can. If you're having a bad day and feeling crabby, you just have to walk away from it. It doesn't make sense to upset the customer, you won't get their business back. You have to take it all in stride.

"How comfortable your job is depends on who you work for. Sometimes management can be a pain, or there are personal conflicts with coworkers. But if you're confident and outgoing, you can deal with it.

"If you don't have enough hours or you're not making enough money, that can be a downside. My hours vary, but usually on Monday and Tuesday I open the store at 9:30 in the morning and I don't leave here until 5. Wednesday I'm off—we go bowling for the Roadhouse Grill at night, we're in a bowling league. That's kind of fun. The general manager is on my team.

Thursday and Friday nights I work from 4 P.M. until midnight. On Sundays I work from five until closing. I get Saturdays off. But at some restaurants you don't get to choose your schedule.

"And you have to really be on a sick bed to call off work. You don't get any sick leave, vacation days, or medical benefits. And the pay for waiters and waitresses is so low; $2.15 an hour doesn't cut it. We have to depend solely on tips, and we also have to claim it for taxes. We can't leave the restaurant until we do that.

"And sometimes you'll have a bad day on tips. You could put in all your hours, but only make $10. But you can make a lot of money if you're good, put your hours in, and stay with it. That's why I'm still doing it after all these years. In a good day I can bring in $100, $120. The problem is, you can't count on it. You never know how much you're going to make.

"An upside is that you can get a job anywhere. And if you know the tricks of the trade, you'll do well. You need to know how to handle people. The first thing is to please the customers and to be hospitable. You have to have an up attitude. Your customers might have had a bad day, and if you're down, that's not going to work. You can try to cheer them up. And often, you end up having pretty good conversations with people that way. I meet a lot of very nice people.

"Another benefit is eating. We don't have to go shopping for food much. We can have all our meals for 50 percent off, with soft drinks for free. And after work, we can put a different shirt on and hang around with coworkers or converse with the customers. They like that.

"I treat my job as if I'm the restaurant owner. I take pride in my work. But if things don't go the way they should, if people are slacking off, for example, I'll be one of the first to mention it. I like to make things better all around.

"I'd like to eventually move up into management, but I don't have the money right now to go back to school. However, in the company I'm with now, there are opportunities for advancement. MIT, they call it. Manager-in-Training. My boss just mentioned something about it. He said I was cut out for this kind of work, that I'm good at it. That was very flattering to hear.

"But the best compliment you can ever get as a waitress is having customers come in and ask for you specifically."

How Laura Got Started

"It was the money. I was in college, taking a secretarial/business course. But I didn't want to sit at a desk and do my boss's job. And I needed to get some money together, so I left school and got a job as a waitress. That was in 1981.

"I've stayed with it for several reasons: the money, I enjoy being around people and serving the public. I'm very outgoing and active and waitressing keeps me in shape."

Expert Advice

"Most people don't look at waitressing as a career. It's something they do to put themselves through school or to hold them over until something else comes along. They come and go a lot.

"But if you enjoy the restaurant business and want to get into management, then that's a different story. Waitressing is a great place to start. Try to do your best, and go out of your way, sometimes, to do extra. Make yourself indispensable. That puts you in better standing with your company. Better hours, better shifts, and ultimately, more money.

"And you need to have an outgoing personality. Just be yourself with your customers."

● ● ●

FOR MORE INFORMATION

Information about careers as restaurant and food service managers, food and beverage servers, chefs, cooks, and other kitchen workers, as well as information how to obtain directories of two- and four-year college programs in restaurant and food service management and shorter courses that will prepare you for other food service careers is available from:

The Educational Foundation of the National Restaurant
   Association
250 South Wacker Drive, Suite 1400
Chicago, IL 60606

Information about certification as a food service management professional is also available from the above address.

General information on hospitality careers may be obtained from:

Council on Hotel, Restaurant, and Institutional Education
1200 17th Street, N.W.
Washington, DC 20036-3097

For information on the American Culinary Federation's apprenticeship and certification programs for cooks, as well as a list of accredited culinary programs, write to:

American Culinary Federation
P.O. Box 3466
St. Augustine, FL 32085

CHAPTER 8 Postal Workers

OVERVIEW

Every day, the U.S. Postal Service receives, sorts, and delivers millions of letters, bills, advertisements, and packages. To do this, it employs about 792,000 workers. Almost five out of ten of these workers are postal clerks, who sort mail and serve customers in post offices, or mail carriers, who deliver the mail.

Clerks and carriers are distinguished by the type of work they do. Clerks are usually classified by the mail processing function they perform, whereas carriers are classified by their type of route city or rural.

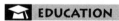 **EDUCATION**
On-the-Job Training Possible

$$$ SALARY/EARNINGS
$20,000 to $40,000

Postal Clerks

There are around 350 mail processing centers throughout the country, which service post offices in surrounding areas and are staffed primarily by postal clerks. Some clerks (commonly referred to as "mail handlers") unload the sacks of incoming mail; separate letters, parcel post, magazines, and newspapers; and transport these to the proper sorting and processing area. In addition, they may load mail into automated letter sorting machines, perform simple canceling operations, and rewrap packages damaged in processing.

After letters have been put through stamp-canceling machines they are taken to other workrooms to be sorted according to destination. Clerks operating older electronic letter-sorting machines push keys corresponding to the ZIP code of the local post office to which each letter will be delivered. The machine then drops the letters into the proper slots. This older, less automated method of letter sorting is being slowly phased out.

Other clerks sort odd-sized letters, magazines, and newspapers by hand. Finally, the mail is sent to local post offices for sorting according to delivery route and delivered.

A growing proportion of clerks operate optical character readers (OCRs) and bar code sorters. Optical character readers read the ZIP code and spray a bar code onto the mail. Bar code sorters then scan the code and sort the mail. Because this is significantly faster than older sorting methods, it is becoming the standard sorting technology in mail processing centers.

Postal clerks at local post offices sort local mail for delivery to individual customers, sell stamps, money orders, postal stationary, and mailing envelopes and boxes, weigh packages to determine postage, and check that packages are in satisfactory condition for mailing. Clerks also register, certify, and insure mail, and answer questions about postage rates, post office boxes, mailing restrictions, and other postal matters. Occasionally, they may help a customer file a claim for a damaged package.

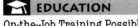 **EDUCATION**
On-the-Job Training Possible

$$$ SALARY/EARNINGS
$20,000 to $40,000

Mail Carriers

Once the mail has been processed and sorted, it is ready to be delivered by mail carriers. The duties of city and rural carriers are very similar. Most carriers travel established routes, delivering and collecting mail. They start work at the post office early in the morning, where they spend a few hours arranging their mail for delivery and taking care of other details. Recently, automated equipment has been able to sort most of the mail for city carriers, allowing them to spend less time sorting and more time delivering mail.

Carriers may cover the route on foot, by vehicle, or a combination of both. On foot, they carry a heavy load of mail in a satchel or push it in a cart. In some urban and most rural areas, they use a car or small truck. Although the Postal Service provides vehicles to city carriers, most rural carriers use their own automobiles. Deliveries are made house-to-house, to roadside mailboxes, and to large buildings, such as offices or apartments, which generally have all the mailboxes on the first floor.

Besides delivering and collecting mail, carriers collect money for postage-due and C.O.D. (cash on delivery) fees and obtain signed receipts for registered, certified, and insured mail. If a customer is not at home, the carrier leaves a notice that tells where special mail is being held.

After completing their routes, carriers return to the post office with mail gathered from street collection boxes, homes, and businesses. They turn in the mail receipts and money collected during the day and may separate letters and parcels for further processing by clerks.

The duties of some city carriers may be very specialized; some deliver only parcel post while others collect mail from street boxes and receiving boxes in office buildings. In contrast, rural carriers provide a wide range of postal services. In addition to delivering and picking up mail, they sell stamps and money orders and accept parcels, letters, and items to be registered, certified, or insured.

All carriers answer customers' questions about postal regulations and services and provide change-of-address cards and other postal forms when requested. In addition to their regularly scheduled duties, carriers often participate in neighborhood service programs, perhaps checking on elderly or shut-in patrons or notifying the police of any suspicious activities along their route.

TRAINING

Postal clerks and mail carriers must be U.S. citizens or have been granted permanent resident-alien status in the United States. They must be at least 18 years old (or 16, if they have a high school diploma). Qualification is based on a written examination that measures speed and accuracy at checking names and numbers, as well as ability to memorize mail distribution procedures. Applicants must pass a physical examination as well, and may be asked to show that they can lift and handle mail sacks weighing up to 70 pounds.

Applicants for jobs as postal clerks operating electronic sorting machines must pass a special examination that includes a machine aptitude test. Applicants for mail carrier positions must have a driver's license, a good driving record, and must achieve a passing grade on a road test.

Applicants should apply at the post office or mail processing center where they wish to work in order to determine when an exam will be given. Applicants' names are listed in order of their examination scores. Five points are added to the score of an honorably discharged veteran, and 10 points to the score of a veteran wounded in combat or disabled.

When a vacancy occurs, the appointing officer chooses one of the top three applicants; the rest of the names remain on the list to be considered for future openings until their eligibility expires (usually two years from the examination date).

Relatively few people under the age of 25 are hired as career postal clerks or mail carriers, a result of keen competition for these jobs and the customary waiting period of one to two years or more after passing the examination. It is not surprising, therefore, that most entrants transfer from other occupations.

New postal clerks and mail carriers are trained on the job by experienced workers. Many post offices offer classroom instruction. Workers receive additional instruction when new equipment or procedures are introduced. They usually are trained by another postal employee or, sometimes, a training specialist hired under contract by the Postal Service.

JOB OUTLOOK

Those seeking a job in the Postal Service can expect to encounter keen competition, as the number of applicants for postal clerk and mail carrier positions is expected to continue to far exceed the number of openings. Job opportunities will vary by occupation and duties performed.

Overall employment of postal clerks is expected to decline through the year 2005. In spite of anticipated increases in the total volume of mail, automation will continue to increase the productivity of postal clerks, slowing employment growth. Increasingly, mail will be moved using automated materials-handling equipment and sorted using optical character readers, bar code sorters, and other automated sorting equipment. In addition, demand for window clerks will be moderated by the increased sales of stamps and other postal products by grocery and department stores and other retail outlets.

Jobs will open up because of the need to replace postal clerks and mail carriers who retire or stop working for other reasons. However, the factors that make entry to these occupations highly competitive–attractive salaries, a good pension plan, job security, and modest educational requirements–contribute to a high degree of job attachment. Accordingly, the need to replace workers is relatively smaller than in other occupations of this size. In contrast to the typical pattern, postal workers generally remain in their jobs until they retire, and relatively few transfer to other occupations.

Although the volume of mail to be processed and delivered rises and falls with the level of business activity, as well as with the season of the year, full-time postal clerks and mail carriers have never been laid off. When mail volume is high, full-time clerks and carriers work overtime, part-time clerks and carriers work additional hours, and casual clerks and carriers may be hired. When mail volume is low, overtime is curtailed, part-timers work fewer hours, and casual workers are discharged.

SALARIES

In 1992 the base pay for beginning full-time carriers and postal clerks was $23,737 a year, rising to a maximum of $33,952 after 12 and a half years of service. Those working between 6 P.M. and 6 A.M. are paid a supplement. Experienced, full-time, city delivery mail carriers earn an average salary of $32,832 a year.

Postal clerks and carriers working part-time flexible schedules begin at $11.81 an hour and, based on the number of years of service, increase to a maximum of $16.91 an hour.

Rural delivery carriers earned average base salaries of $34,951 in 1992. Their earnings are determined through an evaluation of the amount of work required to service their routes. Carriers with heavier workloads generally earn more than those with lighter workloads. Rural carriers also receive an equipment maintenance allowance if they are required to use their own vehicles. In 1992, this was approximately 34 cents per mile.

Postal workers enjoy a variety of employer-provided benefits, including health and life insurance, vacation and sick leave, and a pension plan. And some postal workers receive a uniform allowance, including those workers who are in the public view for four or more hours each day and various maintenance workers. The amount of the allowance depends on the job performed. Some workers are only required to wear a partial uniform, and their allowance is lower.

In 1992, for example, the allowance for a letter carrier was $252 per year, compared to $108 for a window clerk.

Most of these workers belong to one of four unions: American Postal Workers Union, National Association of Letter Carriers, National Postal Mail Handlers Union, and National Rural Letter Carriers Association.

RELATED FIELDS

Other workers whose duties are related to those of window clerks include mail clerks, file clerks, routing clerks, sorters, material moving equipment operators, clerk typists, cashiers, data entry operators, and ticket sellers.

Others with duties related to those of mail carriers include messengers, merchandise deliverers, and delivery-route truck drivers.

INTERVIEW
Elsa Riehl
Window Clerk

Elsa Riehl has been with the post office since 1975. She started in Houston as a letter-sorting machine (LSM) operator, sorting mail at night. She's worked as a sub clerk, unloading and loading trucks and sorting the mail for the carriers, and has been a window clerk since 1993.

What the Job's Really Like

"I'm responsible for selling stamps, taking in packages, and helping customers over the window. I also sort mail for the post office boxes and do special sortings for the large companies, who pay an extra fee to have their mail handled early in the day. Early in the morning I also transport incoming mail from another station to our office.

"I like working with the public. Most of them are pretty easy-going and understanding. I like talking to people and helping them, letting them know what their options are regarding mailing. A lot of people are not aware of the different charges. In other post offices I've seen that a lot of clerks don't explain the services we offer to the customers. I like to be able to explain what Priority mail is, what Express mail is.

"I supervised for a while in Texas and I didn't care for it–I like working with people, I don't like giving the orders. Basically, I like my hours, I like the work itself. I work 6:30 A.M. to 3:30 P.M., Monday through Friday. A lot of times I come in early and stay late. And I get overtime for that. Anything over 8 hours is overtime.

"There's job security, our pensions are good, our salary and benefits are excellent. We can't complain about that, and once we're in, it's very hard to get fired. We're protected through the union.

"But there's a lot of pressure and a lot of downsides to working for the post office. For example, as a window clerk we're responsible for all the stamps we sell. We carry anywhere from $15,000 to $30,000 or $40,000 in stock. We get audited every four months–unless there's a special situation, for example, if a customer complains they were shortchanged. Then we can request a special audit to protect ourselves. We won't open our window the next morning and the auditors will count every single stamp and every penny. If we don't ask for the special audit, we would have to make up the loss at the four month audit. We're only given a $40 leeway. And that's not enough for four months and the amount of money we handle. Above that and it would come out of our own pockets.

"Another problem is that we have no one to answer the phone, to handle customers that call in. Our managers want us, as window clerks, to walk away from our window and answer the phone. That's very hard to do if you're with a customer and you haven't collected the money yet but you've given them the stamps. According to our supervisors, the customer is always right, but what do you do if you come back from the phone and say, 'Well, Ma'am, you haven't paid me,' and the customer says, 'Yes I did.'? Other stations have people to answer the phone and take care of complaints. We're a small office and we don't have that extra staff. The supervisors don't make it easy for us.

"It's not an easy atmosphere. If our upper managers don't get any better and if they don't get someone in there who knows more about window service and delivery, I think in a few years, the way it's going, everyone will be talking about privatization. It's getting to the point where they're giving us supervisors who have no idea what our jobs are. A lot of the people who get promoted, well, it's not *what* they know, it's *who* they know.

"There are problems all throughout the postal service. If you do get a good manager, they tend to move up and out and someone else will come in.

"We're always short-handed. They're aware of the problem, they preach customer service to us, but only when it's convenient for the managers.

"We do occasionally get nasty and arrogant customers, and sometimes it's because we're understaffed. The managers always say to call them and they'll take care of it, but half the time you can't get them over to your station, you can't get them to talk to the customer, and you'll never get them to tell the customer we're understaffed because they don't want to pay the extra overtime to make sure we're staffed properly.

"If you decide to transfer you can lose your seniority. That happened to me when I left Texas and moved to Florida. You keep your years in service and the amount of vacation time you've accrued and retirement benefits, but when I transferred I had 15 years in service and people who had only three were over me in terms of vacation choices and other privileges."

How Elsa Riehl Got Started

"My brother-in-law had worked for the post office for years. I was attending college, studying law enforcement, and looking for part-time work during the upcoming summer break. My brother-in-law suggested I take the postal exam. I took it in April of 1975 and scored 100 percent, which was very unusual. In June I was called for an interview in Houston, Texas. A hurricane was on its way and I drove to the interview with my mother. We were pretty well under water, but I couldn't miss my interview. I went through three different interviews and got hired that same morning.

"The money and benefits were good and I figured I'd just work part-time through the summer. I started nights and went to school part-time during the day, paying my own way. Eventually I finished my degree and got a B.A. in law enforcement from the University of Houston.

"Originally, I had planned to work with juveniles, but there was no money involved there. Even though money wasn't my main interest, I figured that down the line, I'd have to get a master's degree in order to get a decent salary. I talked to a lot of people working in law enforcement, too, and they pretty much talked me out of going for an interview with the police department. I don't regret it. I think I would have gotten too involved. I decided I was happy at the post office. I enjoy my work, I'm pretty content with it."

Expert Advice

"To be honest with you, I'd say come in, do your work, and leave–and hope you enjoy what you're doing. Don't get involved. Too much goes on. There's a lot of favoritism and pressure. There are other jobs that maybe pay a few dollars less but have the same benefits. You'd probably be a lot happier."

INTERVIEW

Nick Delia
Letter Carrier

Nick Delia and his wife are both letter carriers. Nick has been working for the postal service for more than 12 years.

What the Job's Really Like

"You have to rely on your memory a lot in this job. You get to know who is living at a certain address, who's having their mail forwarded. Forwarding the mail is the responsibility of the letter carrier.

"The majority of my route is a business route, which means you're constantly in and out of the truck. For example, the local newspaper is on my route. I pull up to the building, take out their buckets of mail, then take them into the mailroom, then get back into the truck and go to the next stop.

"I start at six o'clock in the morning. When I get in most of the mail is already there. There are other clerks that get in at three or four in the morning. We have to first count our mail. It's counted by the foot. A certain number of letters makes up a foot. They come to you in trays and there's two feet of mail, the letter size, stacked on a tray. Then you've got your magazines and newspapers. You need to know how many feet you have. That's how the amount of time you need to deliver the mail is calculated. In my particular case, 15 feet of mail would equal an 8-hour day. Anything over that, I'd need some overtime hours or some help.

"Then you have to go through all your mail, piece by piece, to check for forwards or holds. After that you have to put the mail into this large case we have, with all sorts of separations. You check the name and the address, then put it into the correct slot. When all your mail is up, you receive your accountable mail and your certified and registered letters. These you have to write up because they have to be signed for by the customer. Then you have your 'mark up mail.' That's the 'moved, left no forwarding address' or 'attempted, addressee unknown.' Then you pull all the mail out of the case—it comes out in the order you'll deliver it. After that, you bundle it up in rubber bands, then you pull out your parcels. Everything then goes out to your truck.

"This all takes about four hours. That's before you get out to the street. I'm usually out on the street by 10 A.M. It looks like the easiest job in the world, but most people have no idea what goes on behind the scenes. The delivery part is the easiest part of the day.

"But, of course you have a lot to deal with on the street. That old saying, 'neither snow, nor sleet,' and all that is really true. It doesn't matter what the weather is, the mail has to go.

"But on the street is really the best part. In my case, I get to talk to a lot of people. You see the same people every day and you get to know them. The mailman really knows a lot abut you. He knows about your family, what you do for a living, where your mail comes from. We know it all. And everybody is always happy to see us. We're like a friend coming to visit.

"We get the opportunity to put in a lot of overtime if we want, maybe even an extra $10,000 a year, and the base top pay for a letter carrier here is pretty good, about $35,400. But we earn our money. It's not every job that you have a dog chasing you down the street or you're working through a lightning storm.

And we have traffic to deal with, and kids running out in the street. We've got our hazards.

"Dealing with management feels like another hazard. Post office management is not known for being too bright, to be honest with you. And a lot of people just don't care about their job. They feel they can't make a difference. It's a government job; they collect their salary and benefits and that's it.

"And there are conflicts and sometimes violence in the post office. It's been in the papers. No one's pulled a gun where I work, but we have our problems.

"But basically, I think it's a good job. I get a feeling of accomplishment on my job. At the beginning of the day there's mail everywhere, but by the end of the day, there's nothing left, it's done. And I enjoy working outside, which is half of the job. I couldn't be a clerk, working indoors all day. The people are friendlier towards the letter carrier than they are to a window clerk."

How Nick Delia Got Started

"I had some family members who were already in the post office. My last job, working for U-Haul, was going nowhere. They were giving the test to work at the post office so I decided to try it. It was basically a memory test, which has a lot to do with the job. I was called and started about 12 years ago."

Expert Advice

"You've got to be physically fit. You've got to enjoy being around other people. It really helps if you're outgoing.

"In addition, this is basically an unskilled job. Of course, you need a good memory and have to be intelligent, but if a person is not inclined to go to college, then this would be a good job."

● ● ●

FOR MORE INFORMATION

Local post offices and state employment service offices can supply details about entrance examinations and specific employment opportunities for postal clerks and mail carriers.

VGM CAREER BOOKS

BUSINESS PORTRAITS
Boeing
Coca-Cola
Ford
McDonald's

CAREER DIRECTORIES
Careers Encyclopedia
Dictionary of Occupational Titles
Occupational Outlook Handbook

CAREERS FOR
Animal Lovers; Bookworms; Caring
People; Computer Buffs; Crafty
People; Culture Lovers;
Environmental Types; Fashion Plates;
Film Buffs; Foreign Language
Aficionados; Good Samaritans;
Gourmets; Health Nuts; History
Buffs; Kids at Heart; Music Lovers;
Mystery Buffs; Nature Lovers; Night
Owls; Number Crunchers; Plant
Lovers; Shutterbugs; Sports Nuts;
Travel Buffs; Writers

CAREERS IN
Accounting; Advertising; Business;
Child Care; Communications;
Computers; Education; Engineering;
the Environment; Finance;
Government; Health Care; High
Tech; Horticulture & Botany;
International Business; Journalism;
Law; Marketing; Medicine; Science;
Social & Rehabilitation Services

CAREER PLANNING
Beating Job Burnout
Beginning Entrepreneur
Big Book of Jobs
Career Planning & Development for
    College Students &
    Recent Graduates
Career Change
Career Success for People with
    Physical Disabilities
Careers Checklists
College and Career Success for Students
    with Learning Disabilities
Complete Guide to Career Etiquette
Cover Letters They Don't Forget
Dr. Job's Complete Career Guide
Executive Job Search Strategies
Guide to Basic Cover Letter Writing
Guide to Basic Résumé Writing
Guide to Internet Job Searching
Guide to Temporary Employment
Job Interviewing for College Students
Joyce Lain Kennedy's Career Book

Out of Uniform
Parent's Crash Course in Career
    Planning
Slame Dunk Résumés
Up Your Grades: Proven Strategies
    for Academic Success

CAREER PORTRAITS
Animals; Cars; Computers;
Electronics; Fashion; Firefighting;
Music; Nature; Nursing; Science;
Sports; Teaching; Travel; Writing

GREAT JOBS FOR
Business Majors
Communications Majors
Engineering Majors
English Majors
Foreign Language Majors
History Majors
Psychology Majors
Sociology Majors

HOW TO
Apply to American Colleges and
    Universities
Approach an Advertising Agency and
    Walk Away with the Job You Want
Be a Super Sitter
Bounce Back Quickly After
    Losing Your Job
Change Your Career
Choose the Right Career
Cómo escribir un currículum vitae en
    inglés que tenga éxito
Find Your New Career Upon
    Retirement
Get & Keep Your First Job
Get Hired Today
Get into the Right Business School
Get into the Right Law School
Get into the Right Medical School
Get People to Do Things Your Way
Have a Winning Job Interview
Hit the Ground Running in Your
    New Job
Hold It All Together When You've
    Lost Your Job
Improve Your Study Skills
Jumpstart a Stalled Career
Land a Better Job
Launch Your Career in TV News
Make the Right Career Moves
Market Your College Degree
Move from College into a
    Secure Job
Negotiate the Raise You Deserve
Prepare Your Curriculum Vitae

Prepare for College
Run Your Own Home Business
Succeed in Advertising When all You
Succeed in College
Succeed in High School
Take Charge of Your Child's Early
    Education
Write a Winning Résumé
Write Successful Cover Letters
Write Term Papers & Reports
Write Your College Application Essay

MADE EASY
College Applications
Cover Letters
Getting a Raise
Job Hunting
Job Interviews
Résumés

**ON THE JOB: REAL PEOPLE
    WORKING IN...**
Communications
Health Care
Sales & Marketing
Service Businesses

OPPORTUNITIES IN
This extensive series provides detailed
    information on more than 150
    individual career fields.

RÉSUMÉS FOR
Advertising Careers
Architecture and Related Careers
Banking and Financial Careers
Business Management Careers
College Students &
    Recent Graduates
Communications Careers
Computer Careers
Education Careers
Engineering Careers
Environmental Careers
Ex-Military Personnel
50+ Job Hunters
Government Careers
Health and Medical Careers
High School Graduates
High Tech Careers
Law Careers
Midcareer Job Changes
Nursing Careers
Re-Entering the Job Market
Sales and Marketing Careers
Scientific and Technical Careers
Social Service Careers
The First-Time Job Hunter

 VGM Career Horizons
a division of *NTC Publishing Group*
4255 West Touhy Avenue
Lincolnwood, Illinois 60646–1975